# BALI TRAVEL GUIDE

*Your Essential Travel Companion for Unforgettable Adventures—Plus 100 Additional Tips and Tricks*

**FRED HUM**

© **Copyright 2023 - All rights reserved.**

The content contained within this book may not be reproduced, duplicated or transmitted without direct written permission from the author or the publisher.

Under no circumstances will any blame or legal responsibility be held against the publisher, or author, for any damages, reparation, or monetary loss due to the information contained within this book, either directly or indirectly.

Legal Notice:

This book is copyright protected. It is only for personal use. You cannot amend, distribute, sell, use, quote or paraphrase any part, or the content within this book, without the consent of the author or publisher.

Disclaimer Notice:

Please note the information contained within this document is for educational and entertainment purposes only. All effort has been executed to present accurate, up to date, reliable, complete information. No warranties of any kind are declared or implied. Readers acknowledge that the author is not engaged in the rendering of legal, financial, medical or professional advice. The content within this book has been derived from various sources. Please consult a licensed professional before attempting any techniques outlined in this book.

By reading this document, the reader agrees that under no circumstances is the author responsible for any losses, direct or indirect, that are incurred as a result of the use of the information contained within this document, including, but not limited to, errors, omissions, or inaccuracies.

# CONTENTS

Introduction .................................................................................... 1
    Bali and Its Wonders ................................................................ 2
    Things to Consider When Traveling to Bali ............................. 3
    What Will This Book Provide You With ................................. 4

Chapter 1: Introduction to Bali ..................................................... 6
    Island of Gods .......................................................................... 6
    Rich History and Culture ......................................................... 7
    Geography and Landscapes ..................................................... 8
    Key Takeaways ........................................................................ 9

Chapter 2: Planning Your Trip ................................................... 10
    Best Time to Visit .................................................................. 10
    Visa and Entry ....................................................................... 10
    Budgeting and Currency ........................................................ 11
    Packing Essentials ................................................................. 12
    Key Takeaways ...................................................................... 12

Chapter 3: Navigating Bali's Regions ........................................ 13
    South Bali: Beaches and Nightlife ......................................... 13
    Central Bali: Ubud and Culture ............................................. 13
    Eastern Bali: Temples and Palaces ........................................ 14
    Western Bali: Parks and Gems .............................................. 15
    Key Takeaways ...................................................................... 16

Chapter 4: Getting Around ............................................................... 17
   Transportation Options ................................................................ 17
   Traffic and Road Etiquette........................................................... 17
   Navigating Roads Safely ............................................................. 18
   Rideshare Apps............................................................................ 18
   Key Takeaways............................................................................ 19

Chapter 5: Cultural Immersion........................................................ 20
   Balinese Spirituality..................................................................... 20
   Arts and Crafts............................................................................. 21
   Festivals and Etiquette ................................................................. 22
   Key Takeaways............................................................................ 22

Chapter 6: Exploring Beaches and Watersports............................... 23
   Iconic Beaches ............................................................................. 23
   Surfing and Diving ...................................................................... 24
   Snorkeling and Water Activities.................................................. 25
   Key Takeaways............................................................................ 26

Chapter 7: Spiritual Journeys .......................................................... 27
   Tanah Lot Temple........................................................................ 27
   Besakih Temple ........................................................................... 28
   Uluwatu and Tirta Empul ............................................................ 28
   Key Takeaways............................................................................ 30

Chapter 8: Ubud—Cultural Haven................................................... 31
   Artistic Legacy............................................................................. 31
   Monkey Forest ............................................................................. 32

Rice Terraces .................................................................... 34

Key Takeaways ................................................................ 35

Chapter 9: Adventures in Nature ............................................ 36

Mount Batur Trek ............................................................ 36

Bali Swing and Jungle ..................................................... 37

Bali Bird Park and Zoo .................................................... 38

Key Takeaways ................................................................ 38

Chapter 10: Island Cuisine .................................................... 39

Balinese Flavors .............................................................. 39

Must-Try Dishes .............................................................. 39

Cooking Classes .............................................................. 41

The Island's Most Popular Restaurants ........................... 42

Key Takeaways ................................................................ 43

Chapter 11: Wellness and Relaxation ..................................... 44

Balinese Spa Traditions ................................................... 44

Wellness Centers ............................................................. 45

Yoga and Meditation ....................................................... 46

Key Takeaways ................................................................ 47

Chapter 12: Shopping and Souvenirs ...................................... 49

Traditional Markets ......................................................... 49

Artisanal Crafts ............................................................... 50

Modern Shopping ............................................................ 51

Key Takeaways ................................................................ 52

Chapter 13: Family-Friendly Fun ............................................ 54

Bali Safari Marine Park ........................................................... 54

Waterbom Bali ......................................................................... 55

Elephant Safari Park ............................................................... 56

Key Takeaways ....................................................................... 58

Chapter 14: Nightlife and Entertainment ..................................... 60

Seminyak's Chic Bars and Clubs ............................................ 60

Legian Street: Pub Crawls and Live Music ............................. 62

Balinese Dance Performances ................................................ 62

Balinese Beach Clubs ............................................................. 63

Key Takeaways ....................................................................... 65

Chapter 15: Beyond Bali—Day Trips and Island-Hopping ........... 67

Nusa Penida: Crystal Bays and Kelingking Beach .................. 67

Lombok: Gili Islands and Mount Rinjani ................................ 68

Java: Borobudur and Prambanan Temples .............................. 69

Key Takeaways ....................................................................... 70

Chapter 16: Accommodation ....................................................... 71

Types of Accommodation Options .......................................... 71

Location Matters ..................................................................... 72

Popular Hotels, Hostels, and Other Accommodation Types Across the Island ..................................................................... 73

Key Takeaways ....................................................................... 73

Chapter 17: Capturing Bali Through Photography ...................... 75

Best Photo Spots ..................................................................... 75

Cultural Sensitivity ................................................................. 76

Key Takeaways ............................................................................. 77
Chapter 18: Safety and Health in Bali ............................................ 79
    Health Precautions and Vaccinations ......................................... 79
    Staying Safe: Common Scams and Local Hazard ..................... 80
    Emergency Contacts and Medical Facilities ............................. 81
    Key Takeaways ............................................................................ 82
Chapter 19: Balinese Language Tips ............................................. 83
    Basic Phrases .............................................................................. 83
    Insights Through Language ........................................................ 84
    Key Takeaways ............................................................................ 84
100 Tips to Consider ..................................................................... 85
References ..................................................................................... 92

# Introduction

Traveling to different places and experiencing new things is an incredible adventure. It opens your mind to new cultures, traditions, and perspectives. Whether you're exploring the busy streets of a vibrant city, hiking through breathtaking natural landscapes, or immersing yourself in local traditions, every destination offers a unique experience. These are the emotions you may experience when visiting Bali.

When you look at the map, you can choose from over a thousand places to visit, but for now, I want to focus on Bali. It is a beautiful island in Indonesia known for its stunning beaches, lush rice terraces, and vibrant culture. It's a paradise for nature lovers and adventure seekers, with opportunities for surfing, diving, and hiking.

The island is also famous for its unique Hindu temples, traditional arts and crafts, and delicious Balinese cuisine. Bali offers an excellent blend of relaxation and excitement, making it a popular destination for travelers from around the world (David, 2023).

Therefore, this book welcomes you to the enchanting island of Bali, where exuberant landscapes, lively traditions, and pristine beaches await. Whether you're seeking spiritual enlightenment, some thrilling adventures, or simply a relaxing getaway, this travel guide is your key to uncovering the hidden gems and must-see attractions of this tropical paradise.

When a person thinks about Bali, they first think about Indonesia, a country located in Southeast Asia. Places like the Maldives, Bora Bora, and Hawaii may come to mind when choosing which tropical island to visit for a vacation getaway. There's no doubt that all these places have something unique to offer, whether it is the natural beauty, the diverse culture, or the delicious cuisines.

However, choosing a place to explore can be quite confusing. It can feel like you're making the biggest decision of your life, and your entire being depends on it. I totally understand; it's super confusing. But don't worry because this book will guide you from A to Z when booking a trip to Bali.

**Bali and Its Wonders**

So, what does this beautiful, awe-inspiring island have to offer? Let's dive right into it. Bali is truly a treasure trove of diverse attractions, rich culture, and unique charm. From the legendary rice terraces of Tegalalang to the majestic temples like Uluwatu and Tanah Lot, the island is adorned with breathtaking landscapes that will leave you in awe (Shell, 2023).

The vibrant arts scene in Ubud showcases traditional Balinese dance and music performances, while the bustling markets offer a glimpse into the local craftsmanship and vibrant textiles. Moreover, Bali's spiritual side is evident in the numerous temples and sacred sites, such as the serene Pura Besakih, known as the *Mother Temple.*

For adventure seekers, Bali offers thrilling activities like surfing in Kuta, diving in the crystal-clear waters of Nusa Penida, and hiking up Mount Batur to catch the stunning sunrise. The island's unique charm lies in its warm and welcoming people, who embrace their traditions and customs with pride.

Balinese ceremonies and festivals, like the exuberant Galungan and Nyepi, provide an opportunity to witness the island's deep-rooted spirituality and sense of community. Whether you're exploring the vibrant streets of Seminyak, indulging in a traditional Balinese massage, or savoring the flavors of local cuisine like Nasi Goreng and Babi Guling, Bali promises an unforgettable experience that will capture your heart and leave you longing for more.

So, what are you waiting for? Book a trip to the beautiful island of Bali and find yourself among all the magical things it has to offer. It will definitely be a trip of a lifetime.

## Things to Consider When Traveling to Bali

When preparing for a trip to Bali, there are several important factors to keep in mind. First and foremost, check the visa requirements for your country of residence and ensure that your passport is valid for at least six months beyond your intended departure date.

It's also essential to research and decide on the best time to visit Bali, taking into account elements such as weather, peak tourist seasons, and any major cultural events or holidays that may affect your travel plans. However, if you are confused, continue reading this book to find out when is the perfect time to visit.

Additionally, packing wisely is crucial for a comfortable and enjoyable trip. Bali's tropical climate means that lightweight and breathable clothing is a must. Pack plenty of swimwear, as the island boasts beautiful beaches and opportunities for water activities.

Don't forget to bring sunscreen, insect repellent, a hat, and sunglasses to protect yourself from the sun's rays. Furthermore, it's a good idea to pack a reusable bottle to remain hydrated while exploring the island. Moreover, respecting the local customs and traditions is key when visiting Bali.

The predominant religion in Bali is Hinduism, and there are numerous temples and sacred sites throughout the island. When entering these places, it is important to dress modestly, covering your shoulders and knees. Be mindful of your behavior and avoid any disrespectful actions. It's also considered polite to learn a few basic phrases in Bahasa Indonesia, the local language, such as greetings—*salam*—and thank you—*terima kasih*.

In addition, remember that safety is paramount when traveling to any destination, and Bali is no exception. While the island is generally safe, it's always wise to take precautions. Be cautious of your belongings and avoid displaying expensive items that may attract unwanted attention.

Use reliable transportation options and be aware of your surroundings, especially in crowded areas. It's also advisable to have travel insurance that covers medical emergencies and trip cancellations. The island of Bali is renowned for its delicious cuisine, and trying local dishes is a must-do.

The flavors of Balinese food are diverse and tantalizing. However, it's important to be mindful of food hygiene and choose reputable establishments for dining. Drinking bottled water is recommended to prevent any potential stomach issues.

Lastly, embrace the vibrant Balinese culture and immerse yourself in the island's unique experiences. Attend a traditional dance performance, participate in a cooking class, or visit local markets to get a taste of the authentic Balinese way of life. Engaging with the local community and showing respect for their customs will enhance your overall travel experience.

**What Will This Book Provide You With**

This *Bali Travel Guide* will cover essential information about the island, including popular tourist attractions, recommended accommodations, transportation options, local customs, and traditions, as well as tips for exploring Bali's natural beauty and experiencing its rich cultural heritage.

Moreover, it will provide insights into the best times to visit, local cuisine recommendations, and suggestions for off-the-beaten-path destinations. As readers, you will be able to take away valuable insights and knowledge about Bali's top attractions, hidden gems, and cultural experiences.

You will have a comprehensive understanding of the island's unique customs, etiquette, and traditions. The travel guide will provide practical tips on navigating transportation, finding accommodations, and exploring Bali's natural wonders. Overall, as readers, I hope you will feel well-prepared and excited to embark on your Balinese adventure!

Therefore, be prepared to immerse yourself in the rich culture, indulge in delicious food, and embark on unforgettable journeys across Bali's diverse landscapes. Let's begin this unforgettable adventure together.

# CHAPTER 1

# Introduction to Bali

Bali is a magical island that has an abundance of things to offer. But apart from the fact that the island is known to be a tropical paradise, it has a rich history that makes it much more interesting.

**Island of Gods**

Bali, known as the Island of Gods, is a tropical paradise that enthralls visitors with its enchanting beauty and rich spiritual heritage. This Indonesian island is renowned for its vibrant culture, breathtaking landscapes, and deep-rooted religious traditions.

One of the main reasons why Bali is called the Island of Gods is its strong connection to Hinduism. The majority of the Balinese population practices Balinese Hinduism, a unique blend of Hinduism, Buddhism, and Animism. The island is dotted with thousands of temples, shrines, and sacred sites, each dedicated to a specific deity or spiritual concept. These temples serve as a focal point for religious ceremonies, rituals, and offerings, creating a palpable sense of spirituality that permeates the island (Putradana, 2022).

Beyond its religious significance, Bali is also known for its natural beauty. The locals believe the gods and goddesses have blessed Bali with this natural abundance, making it a place of divine beauty. The island is renowned for its exquisite craftsmanship, including intricate wood carvings, colorful textiles, and traditional Balinese dance and music.

These artistic expressions are believed to be inspired by the gods and serve as a way to honor and connect with The Divine. The spiritual essence of Bali can be felt in every aspect of daily life. The Balinese people are deeply devoted to their religious practices and rituals, which are woven into their daily routines.

## Rich History and Culture

Bali's rich history and culture are truly fascinating. This Indonesian island has a vibrant heritage that spans thousands of years. From ancient kingdoms to colonial influences, Bali's history has shaped its unique cultural identity. The island's history is intertwined with Hinduism, which arrived in Bali around the first century [C.E.] (*Bali - History and Culture*, n.d.).

The influence of Hinduism can be seen in the magnificent temples and religious ceremonies that are an integral part of Balinese life. The influence of various foreign powers has also shaped Bali. The island was ruled by various dynasties, including the Majapahit Empire, which brought significant cultural and artistic developments to Bali.

Later, Bali came under Dutch colonial rule, which left its mark on the island's architecture and governance. As a result, the cultural traditions of Bali are deeply rooted in its history. The island is known for its vibrant arts scene, including traditional dance, music, and visual arts.

Another important aspect of Balinese culture is the concept of *Tri Hita Karana*, which highlights the euphony between humans, nature, and the spiritual realm. This philosophy permeates every aspect of Balinese life, from the design of traditional houses to the cultivation of rice fields.

Bali's rich history and culture continue to thrive today, attracting visitors from all over the world who are captivated by the island's beauty and spiritual essence. Exploring Bali's historical sites, witnessing traditional ceremonies, and immersing oneself in the local customs offer a deep appreciation for the island's cultural heritage.

## Geography and Landscapes

Bali's landscape and geography are as diverse and breathtaking as its rich history and culture. This Indonesian paradise is renowned for its stunning natural beauty and varied terrain. The island is home to several volcanoes, including Mount Agung and Mount Batur, which add to the dramatic scenery (*Bali Geography*, n.d.).

These volcanic mountains not only provide incredible views but also offer opportunities for adventurous hikes and sunrise treks. Additionally, Bali is blessed with beautiful beaches that stretch along its coastline. From the popular Kuta Beach to the serene shores of Nusa Dua, there is a beach for every preference. The crystal-clear waters and pristine white sands make Bali a haven for sun-seekers and water sports enthusiasts.

Inland Bali's landscape is adorned with emerald-green rice terraces, which are an indication of the island's agricultural heritage. These terraces, known as *subak*, are visually stunning and important to Bali's traditional farming practices.

Bali's geography also includes dense tropical forests and jungles, where exotic flora and fauna thrive. Exploring these natural wonders offers a chance to encounter rare wildlife and immerse oneself in the tranquility of nature.

**Key Takeaways**

Bali is known as the Island of Gods because of the local's connection with religion.

The Balinese people are very spiritually connected.

Bali has a rich history and culture because of its links to the ancient kingdoms.

The island's culture is one of the main tourist attractions.

Bali has a very unique landscape ranging from volcanoes to beaches.

# CHAPTER 2

# Planning Your Trip

If it's not already obvious, Bali is known for its mesmerizing beaches, mountains, rice fields, and buzzing tourist-attracting features. It has all the types of places to visit that tourists are appealed by. As the island has so much to offer, planning a trip to Bali is super exciting!

**Best Time to Visit**

The perfect time to visit Bali is during the dry season, typically from April to September. This period offers plenty of sunshine and lower rain chances, making it ideal for outdoor activities and exploring the island's stunning beaches. However, remember that this is also the peak season for tourists, so expect larger crowds and much higher prices (Cook, 2023).

If you prefer a more peaceful and quieter experience, consider visiting Bali during the months of April–May or September–October. You can still enjoy good weather while avoiding the peak tourist rush during these times. It will also be lighter on your pocket, but the experience may be slightly inferior to the dry season.

**Visa and Entry**

Regarding flights, compare prices from different airlines to find the best deal. Booking a trip in advance can also save you money. Naturally, late bookings are always pricier. Of course, when planning a trip, you must apply for a visa to visit Bali–Indonesia, unless you have a passport from one of the countries on the Visa Exemption Arrangement (VEA) list (Michael, 2022). Some countries that don't need a visa include Brunei, Malaysia, The Philippines, Thailand, Myanmar, and many more.

If you do not belong to one of these countries, you can enter Bali and apply for a Visa on Arrival (VOA) before coming if you are on the VOA-approved countries list. An excellent alternative to the VOA is a Single Entry Visa, which is valid for 60 days and can be renewed twice for a total possible stay of 180 days.

**Budgeting and Currency**

Next, set a budget for your trip. Determine how much you're willing to spend on flights, accommodation, activities, and meals. This will help you make decisions that fit within your financial means. When it comes to budgeting for a trip to Bali, it's important to consider both the cost of living and your personal preferences. Bali offers a huge range of accommodation options, from budget-friendly hostels to luxurious resorts.

Furthermore, food and transportation can vary in price, depending on where you choose to eat and how you get around. It's a good idea to set a daily budget for meals, activities, and transportation and stick to it as closely as possible. As for currency, the official currency of Bali is the Indonesian Rupiah (IDR).

*Bali Travel Guide*

## Packing Essentials

When packing for your trip to Bali, there are a few essentials you shouldn't forget. First, make sure to pack lightweight and breathable clothing, as Bali's climate is tropical and can be quite hot and humid. Don't forget to bring swimwear, as you'll want to dip in Bali's beautiful beaches and pools (*Pack Your Bags*, n.d.).

Additionally, sunscreen is a must to protect your skin from the strong sun rays, along with a hat and sunglasses. Mosquito repellent is also important to ward off those pesky insects. Moreover, bring a travel adapter to charge your devices, as the electrical outlets in Bali may be different from your home country.

## Key Takeaways

Traveling between April and September will provide the best weather for the trip.

You will need a visa to travel to Bali unless your country is exempt from requiring one.

Save some money for your trip and get the currency exchanged for the Indonesian Rupiah.

Make sure to pack light and summery clothes for when you choose to travel.

# CHAPTER 3

# Navigating Bali's Regions

The island of Bali is divided into five regions: the Northern, Southern, Eastern, Western, and Central regions. All of these areas have something unique that stands out and attracts tourists and visitors.

**South Bali: Beaches and Nightlife**

South Bali is an absolute paradise for beach enthusiasts and night owls. The region is renowned for its beaches and vibrant nightlife, creating a perfect blend of relaxation and excitement. South Bali boasts a plethora of stunning beaches that cater to all preferences. From the lively and bustling Kuta Beach, where you can catch some waves or simply soak up the sun, to the trendy and upscale Seminyak Beach, with its luxurious beach clubs and picturesque sunset views, there is a beach for everyone (Hajra, n.d.).

The crystal-clear waters and pristine sands make these beaches a true tropical paradise. When the sun sets, South Bali comes alive with an electric nightlife scene. The streets of Kuta, Seminyak, and Legian are lined with various bars, clubs, and restaurants, offering a diverse range of entertainment options. Whether tourists are in the mood for live music, DJ sets, or simply enjoying delicious cuisine, the nightlife in South Bali has something to suit every taste.

**Central Bali: Ubud and Culture**

Central Bali, particularly the enchanting town of Ubud, is a cultural gem that presents a unique and immersive experience. Ubud is known for its rich artistic heritage, traditional crafts, and spiritual practices. The town is home to the famous Ubud Palace, where tourists can witness traditional dance performances that show the beauty and grace of Balinese culture.

To better understand Balinese spirituality, visit the sacred Monkey Forest Sanctuary, where you can watch playful monkeys and ancient temples nestled amidst greenery. Moreover, in Central Bali lies the Tegalalang Rice Terraces, a breathtaking landscape that showcases the intricate irrigation system and the beauty of traditional rice cultivation.

Ubud is also a hub for wellness and yoga retreats, offering a serene and peaceful environment to rejuvenate the mind, body, and soul. Explore the local markets to discover unique handicrafts, textiles, and jewelry that reflect the region's rich cultural heritage.

## Eastern Bali: Temples and Palaces

Eastern Bali is a treasure trove of ancient temples and majestic palaces that showcase the island's rich cultural heritage. One of the most iconic temples in Eastern Bali is the Besakih Temple, also known as the *Mother Temple*. Perched on the slopes of Mount Agung, this sacred site is considered the holiest and largest temple complex in Bali (Charlotte, 2023).

Its grandeur and spiritual significance make it a must-visit destination for those seeking a deeper understanding of Balinese Hinduism. Another gem in Eastern Bali is the Tirta Gangga Water Palace, a stunning area of pools, fountains, and gardens. Built by the royal family of Karangasem, this palace is a feast for the eyes and a place of tranquility and serenity.

Tourists can also visit the Goa Lawah Temple, also known as the *Bat Cave Temple*. This unique temple is built around a cave inhabited by thousands of bats and is believed to be a protective shrine against evil spirits.

## Northern Bali: Volcanoes and Retreats

Northern Bali is a haven for nature lovers and those seeking tranquility. One of the prominent volcanoes in this region is Mount Batur.

This active volcano provides a mesmerizing backdrop for outdoor enthusiasts who embark on the sunrise trek to its summit.

Witnessing the sunrise from the top of Mount Batur is an unforgettable experience that rewards you with panoramic views of the surrounding landscape. On the other hand, the town of Lovina is another gem in Northern Bali, known for its black sand beaches and dolphin sightings. Visitors can take a boat ride at sunrise to witness these jolly creatures in their natural habitat.

**Western Bali: Parks and Gems**

Western Bali is a treasure trove of natural parks and hidden jewels waiting to be discovered. One of the must-visit parks in Western Bali is West Bali National Park. This protected area is home to diverse plants, including the endangered Bali Starling. You can hike through its trails, go bird-watching, or even embark on a thrilling wildlife safari (Conn, 2023).

For a unique experience, visitors can head to Menjangan Island, located off the coast of Western Bali. This small island is part of the West Bali National Park and offers incredible snorkeling and diving opportunities. Similarly, you can make your way to Pemuteran. This serene coastal village is known for its beautiful beaches and the Pemuteran Bay Coral Project, where you can participate in coral reef restoration efforts.

*Bali Travel Guide*

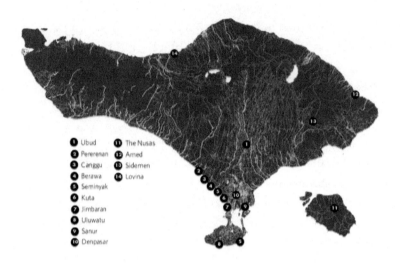

## Key Takeaways

Northern, Southern, Eastern, Western, and Central Bali have a lot of magnificent things to offer.

Whether it is partying, swimming, diving, watching monkeys, or visiting temples, Bali has it all.

Tourists can visit all the geographical locations to experience everything or focus on one region according to their interests.

CHAPTER 4

# Getting Around

When traveling to a new city or country, getting to know how to travel is crucial. Whether it be through local transport or finding the equivalent of an Uber, knowing how to get from point A to point B is imperative.

**Transportation Options**

Bali offers a variety of transportation options to explore the island's beauty. One popular choice is hiring a scooter, which allows you to navigate through traffic and reach hidden gems. If you prefer a more relaxed experience, taxis and ride-sharing services are readily available. They provide convenient and comfortable rides, especially for longer distances (Matt, n.d.).

For a unique cultural experience, you can opt for a traditional *bemo*, a small minivan that operates as a shared public transport. It's a great way to interact with locals and immerse yourself in the local culture. Additionally, private car rentals with drivers are popular for those who want flexibility and convenience.

These drivers can also double as tour guides, providing valuable insights into Bali's history and attractions. Lastly, if you're traveling with a larger group, consider hiring a van or minibus to accommodate everyone comfortably.

**Traffic and Road Etiquette**

Regarding traffic and road etiquette in Bali, being prepared for a unique experience is key. The roads can be quite busy, especially in popular tourist areas like Kuta or Seminyak. Traffic can sometimes be challenging, with scooters, cars, and pedestrians all sharing the road. Staying alert and patient while navigating through traffic is essential.

In terms of road etiquette, it's customary to use your horn as a signal to other drivers, whether to indicate your presence or to say thank you. Remember that the traffic rules may differ from what you're used to, so it's a good idea to familiarize yourself with local driving customs before hitting the road (Marlin, 2023).

Remember to drive carefully and be cautious of your surroundings. Also, be considerate of pedestrians and give them the right of way when necessary. By being mindful of the traffic and following the local road etiquette, you can have a safe and enjoyable journey exploring the beautiful island of Bali.

**Navigating Roads Safely**

Road safety is crucial when navigating the streets of Bali. To ensure a safe journey, you can take several precautions. First and foremost, always wear a helmet if you're riding a scooter or motorcycle. This will protect you in case of an accident. Secondly, obey the traffic rules and signals, even if others around you are not following them.

Stay focused and be aware of other drivers, especially when changing lanes or making turns. Keep a safe distance from the vehicle in front of you to allow for sudden stops or maneuvers. Avoid distractions like using your mobile while driving, which can impair your focus and reaction time.

Lastly, be mindful of the road conditions, as some areas may have potholes or uneven surfaces. Adjust your speed accordingly and be prepared for unexpected obstacles. By being vigilant, following traffic rules, and prioritizing safety, you can enjoy your time exploring Bali while minimizing the risks on the road.

**Rideshare Apps**

Ride-sharing in Bali is a convenient and popular option for getting around the island. Services like Gojek and Grab are widely available and offer affordable transportation solutions. Whether you need a quick ride to your hotel, want to explore different attractions, or simply want to avoid the hassle of driving and parking, ride-sharing apps can be a great choice (Caf, 2023).

Just download the app, input your destination, and a driver will pick you up in no time. It's vital to note that ride-sharing services may not be available in all areas of Bali, especially in more remote locations. Additionally, during peak hours or busy tourist seasons, it's possible to face longer wait times or higher prices.

To guarantee a smooth experience, ensure a stable internet connection and charge your phone. Always double-check the driver's details and license plate before getting into the vehicle; for your safety.

**Key Takeaways**

Public transport or local scooters is a quick and cheap way to travel around the island.

Remember to follow the rules while on the road and not worry about any driver or pedestrian.

Apps such as Gojek or Grab can be used to travel longer distances.

# CHAPTER 5

# Cultural Immersion

Balinese culture has a lot of history and value. It is one of the main things that tourists go to Bali for and get a knowledgeable experience when they learn even more about what the island has to offer.

**Balinese Spirituality**

Balinese spirituality is deeply rooted in the island's unique cultural and religious practices. Balinese people follow a form of Hinduism known as Balinese Hinduism, which combines elements of Hinduism, Buddhism, and Animism. Spirituality is an integral part of daily life in Bali, with rituals and ceremonies playing a significant role. Temples, known as *puras*, are scattered throughout the island and serve as important spiritual centers (Turtle, 2023).

In this setting, Balinese people believe in the presence of gods, spirits, and ancestors and strive to maintain a harmonious relationship with them. Offerings, known as *canang sari*, are made daily to honor and appease these spiritual beings. Balinese spirituality also emphasizes the balance between good and evil forces, with rituals performed to maintain this equilibrium.

The island is filled with sacred sites, such as Mount Agung and Tirta Empul, where people go to seek purification and spiritual enlightenment. Balinese spirituality is not just confined to religious practices but also woven into various aspects of daily life, including art, dance, and music. It is a beautiful and rich tradition that adds a sense of mysticism and reverence to the island's vibrant culture.

**Arts and Crafts**

The arts and crafts in Bali are a true reflection of the island's rich cultural heritage. Balinese artisans are known for their exceptional skills and attention to detail, creating exquisite pieces that showcase their creativity and craftsmanship. Note that wood carving is a prominent art form in Bali, with intricate sculptures depicting mytholog-figures, deities, and everyday scenes.

Furthermore, the art of batik, a traditional Indonesian textile technique, is widely practiced in Bali. Batik fabrics are adorned with intricate patterns and vibrant colors, representing the island's cultural motifs and stories. Silver and gold jewelry making is another significant craft in Bali, with skilled artisans crafting intricate pieces featuring traditional Balinese designs.

In addition, painting is highly regarded, with styles ranging from traditional Balinese art to contemporary and abstract works. Balinese arts and crafts are not just limited to visual arts but also extend to music, dance, and theater. Traditional Balinese dance performances, such as the Barong dance and Legong dance, are a captivating blend of movement, storytelling, and vibrant costumes. The arts and crafts in Bali celebrate the island's cultural identity and provide a glimpse into the artistic soul of the Balinese people.

**Festivals and Etiquette**

Festivals in Bali are vibrant and colorful celebrations that showcase the island's rich cultural traditions. One of the most important festivals is Nyepi, also known as the Day of Silence. During Nyepi, the entire island comes to a complete halt as people observe silence, meditation, and self-reflection (Julie, 2022).

Another significant festival is Galungan, which commemorates the victory of good over evil. Decorative bamboo poles, known as *penjor*, line the streets, and families come together to offer prayers and make offerings. The Kite Festival, held annually in July, is a sight to behold, with colorful kites filling the sky.

Balinese etiquette is deeply rooted in respect and politeness. When visiting temples, it's important to dress modestly and wear a sarong and sash. It is customary to greet others with a smile and a slight bow, and it is considered impolite to point with your finger. When receiving or giving something, using your right hand or both hands is polite. Balinese people appreciate visitors who show interest in their culture and customs.

**Key Takeaways**

Balinese people are very in tune with their spirituality and hold it close to their hearts.

Arts and culture are an important part of their society, and they enjoy taking part in them.

The Balinese focus on etiquette during their festivals as it is a significant part of their culture.

# CHAPTER 6

# Exploring Beaches and Watersports

Apart from the great history and culture of Bali, the landscape is one that is absolutely stunning. The island is known for its beautiful beaches and the plethora of watersports that come along with it.

**Iconic Beaches**

Bali is renowned for its breathtaking beaches that attract visitors from all over the world. One of the most iconic beaches is Kuta Beach, known for its golden sands and world-class surf breaks. It's a vibrant spot where you can enjoy the sun, catch some waves, or simply relax and soak up the beach vibes. Another popular beach is Seminyak Beach, famous for its upscale resorts, trendy beach clubs, and stunning sunsets (Louise, 2023).

If you're looking for a more secluded and tranquil experience, head to Nusa Dua Beach. With its crystal-clear waters and pristine white sand, it's the perfect place to unwind and enjoy the serenity. For those seeking adventure and natural beauty, visit Uluwatu Beach. Located on the Bukit Peninsula, it offers breathtaking cliffside views and is a popular spot for surfing and exploring hidden caves. And let's not forget about the picturesque Jimbaran Beach, known for its seafood restaurants and romantic atmosphere. Whether you're a sun seeker, a surfer, or simply a beach lover, Bali's iconic beaches offer something for everyone.

## Surfing and Diving

Bali is a paradise for both surfers and divers alike. The island boasts world-class surf breaks and stunning dive sites that cater to all experience levels. For surfers, Uluwatu is a must-visit destination. It offers powerful and consistent waves that attract surfers from around the globe. Another popular surf spot is Padang Padang, known for its hollow barrels and challenging breaks.

If you're a beginner, Canggu is a great place to start, with its mellow waves and surf schools offering lessons. When it comes to diving, Bali offers an underwater wonderland. Tulamben is famous for the USAT Liberty shipwreck, where you can explore the coral-covered remains and encounter a diverse array of marine life. Nusa Penida is another diving hotspot known for its crystal-clear waters and encounters with majestic manta rays.

For those seeking a unique experience, the underwater temple garden in Pemuteran is a must-see. It's like diving into a magical world with vibrant coral structures and statues. Whether you're riding the waves or exploring the depths of the ocean, Bali's surf and dive scenes will leave you in awe.

**Snorkeling and Water Activities**

When it comes to snorkeling and water activities, Bali has got you covered. The island is a haven for underwater enthusiasts, offering a superabundance of vibrant coral reefs and diverse marine life. One of the top snorkeling spots is Amed, located on the east coast of Bali. Here, you can explore the stunning Japanese Shipwreck and encounter colorful tropical fish up close.

Another popular destination is Menjangan Island, part of West Bali National Park. Its crystal-clear waters and thriving coral gardens make it an ideal spot for snorkeling. If you're looking for a unique experience, head to Nusa Lembongan and Nusa Penida. These neighboring islands offer breathtaking snorkeling opportunities to swim alongside majestic manta rays and explore vibrant coral reefs.

Bali offers options like jet skiing, parasailing, and banana boat rides for those seeking more adventurous water activities. Whether you're a snorkeling enthusiast or an adrenaline junkie, Bali's waters are waiting to be explored and enjoyed!

**Key Takeaways**

Apart from a lot of sightseeing places, Bali has a bunch of fun activities in which tourists can take part.

There are a lot of water-related activities, such as snorkeling, waterboarding, and surfing.

Water enthusiasts really have their work set out for them with the abundance of activities they can enjoy.

# CHAPTER 7

# Spiritual Journeys

Bali is famous for its spiritual journeys because of its rich Balinese spirituality, rituals, and ceremonies. The unique blend of Hinduism and local beliefs in Bali creates a vibrant and spiritual atmosphere that attracts many seekers worldwide.

**Tanah Lot Temple**

This temple is one of the most iconic and picturesque temples in Bali. Located on a rocky outcrop along the Southwestern coast of Bali, this temple is known for its stunning sunset views. The name *Tanah Lot* means *land in the sea* in Balinese, perfectly describing the temple's unique location. The temple is perched on a large rock formation, surrounded by the Indian Ocean, which creates a dramatic and mesmerizing sight (Gunadi, n.d.).

The Tanah Lot Temple holds great spiritual significance for the Balinese people. It is believed to be a sacred place of worship and is dedicated to the sea gods. Tourists can explore the temple complex and witness the intricate Balinese architecture. The temple is adorned with traditional stone carvings and sculptures, showcasing the rich cultural heritage of Bali.

It is possible to walk across to the temple during low tide, but during high tide, the temple appears to be floating on the water. This adds to the mystical allure of the Tanah Lot Temple. The temple complex also features smaller shrines, beautiful gardens, and a market where visitors can purchase souvenirs and local handicrafts.

In addition to its spiritual significance, this temple offers breathtaking views of the ocean and the surrounding coastline. Many visitors flock to this site to witness the magical sunset, as the golden hues paint the sky and reflect off the shimmering waters.

**Besakih Temple**

This temple, also known as the *Mother Temple of Bali*, is a majestic and significant Hindu temple complex situated on the slopes of Mount Agung. It is considered the most important temple in Bali and holds great spiritual significance for the Balinese people. The temple complex consists of over 80 temples dedicated to different deities and representing various aspects of the Hindu faith.

Besakih Temple is a religious site and a cultural and architectural masterpiece. Its towering pagodas, intricate stone carvings, and ornate gateways are a testament to the rich artistic heritage of Bali. The temple's strategic location offers breathtaking views of the surrounding landscapes, including lush rice terraces and the majestic Mount Agung.

Visiting the Besakih Temple provides a profound spiritual experience, as you can witness the Balinese people engaging in their religious rituals and ceremonies. Moreover, the temple complex is a hub of activity during important Hindu festivals, such as Galungan and Kuningan, when devotees come to pay their respects and seek blessings.

Whether you are a spiritual seeker, an architecture enthusiast, or simply curious about Balinese culture, a visit to the Besakih Temple is a must. It offers a glimpse into the deep-rooted spirituality and cultural traditions that make Bali such a unique and enchanting destination.

**Uluwatu and Tirta Empul**

Uluwatu is a stunning coastal area in Bali known for its magnificent cliffs and breathtaking ocean views. It is home to the Uluwatu Temple, which sits on top of a steep cliff overlooking the Indian Ocean.

The temple is a place of worship and a popular spot to witness magical sunsets and traditional Balinese dance performances (*A Guide to the Holy Springs*, n.d.).

Tirta Empul, on the other hand, is a sacred water temple located in the village of Tampaksiring. It is famous for its holy spring water, believed to have healing properties. Visitors can take part in a purification ritual by bathing in the sacred pools and experiencing the spiritual cleansing process.

Both Uluwatu and Tirta Empul offer unique cultural and spiritual experiences that showcase the beauty and traditions of Bali. Whether you're seeking natural wonders or spiritual enlightenment, these destinations are sure to leave a lasting impression on your journey through the island.

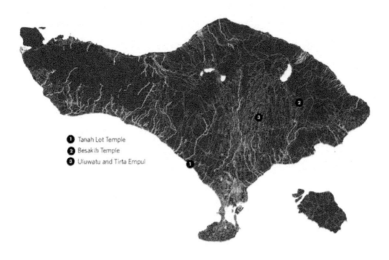

**Key Takeaways**

The island is home to numerous temples, such as Besakih Temple and Uluwatu Temple.

People in Bali can connect with their spirituality and experience a sense of peace and tranquility.

Tourists can visit a lot of temples in Bali and get religious insights into what they have to offer.

# CHAPTER 8

# Ubud—Cultural Haven

Ubud is truly a cultural haven in Bali. It's a place where art, tradition, and spirituality come together in perfect harmony. Ubud is known for its vibrant arts scene, with numerous galleries, workshops, and craft markets showcasing the talents of local artisans.

**Artistic Legacy**

Bali has a rich and vibrant artistic legacy deeply rooted in its culture. The island is known for its exquisite craftsmanship, intricate sculptures, colorful paintings, and mesmerizing dance performances. Balinese art reflects the island's spiritual beliefs and close connection to nature. The artistic traditions have been passed down through generations, preserving the unique cultural heritage of Bali (Rose, 2023).

One of the most prominent art forms in Bali is traditional dance, such as the famous Barong dance and Legong dance. These dances tell stories from Hindu epics and are performed with graceful movements and elaborate costumes. Balinese painting is another significant aspect of the artistic legacy, with its distinct style characterized by intricate details, vibrant colors, and mythological themes.

The island is also renowned for its wood carving and stone carving. Balinese artisans create stunning sculptures of gods, demons, and mythical creatures, showcasing their exceptional skill and creativity. The artistry extends beyond visual arts, as Balinese music and gamelan orchestras play a vital role in religious ceremonies and cultural events.

The artistic legacy in Bali continues to thrive and evolve, with contemporary artists blending traditional techniques with modern influences. Galleries and art spaces in Ubud and Seminyak showcase the talents of local and international artists, providing a platform for artistic expression and cultural exchange.

Bali's artistic legacy is a testament to the island's rich cultural heritage and enduring passion for creativity. It serves as a source of inspiration and pride for the Balinese people and attracts visitors worldwide who appreciate the beauty and depth of Balinese art.

**Monkey Forest**

The Monkey Forest in Bali is a must-visit destination for nature and animal lovers. Located in Ubud, this enchanting sanctuary houses many long-tailed macaques. The forest is a lush and serene environment, with towering trees, ancient temples, and winding pathways.

Visitors can observe these playful monkeys in their natural habitat as they swing from branches, interact with each other, and even approach visitors for food. It's important to follow the guidelines provided by the park to ensure a safe and respectful experience for both humans and monkeys.

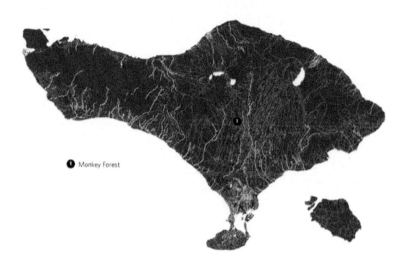

Aside from the monkeys, the Monkey Forest is also a cultural and spiritual site. It houses three ancient Hindu temples, each with unique architecture and significance. The Pura Dalem Agung, or the Great Temple of Death, is particularly awe-inspiring with its intricate carvings and statues.

Exploring the Monkey Forest offers a chance to connect with nature, witness the playful antics of monkeys, and immerse oneself in the spiritual ambiance of the temples. It's an experience that combines wildlife, culture, and natural beauty, making it a highlight of any trip to Bali.

## Rice Terraces

The rice terraces in Bali are a true testament to the island's natural beauty and agricultural heritage. These terraces are carefully sculpted into the hillsides, creating a stunning landscape of cascading green fields. They showcase the intricate and sustainable irrigation system known as *subak*, which has been passed down through generations.

The most famous rice terraces in Bali are in Tegalalang, where visitors can take in panoramic views and even walk through the terraces themselves. The greenery, the rice paddies' rhythmic pattern, and the flowing water sound create a serene and picturesque atmosphere.

Exploring the rice terraces allows you to immerse yourself in the traditional agricultural practices of Bali and appreciate the harmony between nature and human cultivation. It's a truly awe-inspiring experience that will leave you with a deep appreciation for the island's cultural and natural heritage.

**Key Takeaways**

Ubud is home to numerous temples and sacred sites where you can witness Balinese ceremonies and rituals.

The lush surroundings of Ubud, with its rice terraces and jungles, provide the perfect backdrop for a spiritual journey or a peaceful retreat.

Whether you're seeking artistic inspiration, cultural immersion, or a deeper connection with Balinese spirituality, Ubud is the place to be.

## CHAPTER 9

# Adventures in Nature

When visiting Bali, the locals, along with the tourists, can experience great adventures in nature. There are various activities for individuals to take part in and spend their time trying something new.

**Mount Batur Trek**

The Mount Batur trek is an absolute must-do for adventure enthusiasts visiting Bali. It's an opportunity to hike up an active volcano and witness the stunning sunrise from its summit.

The trek starts early in the morning, allowing you to experience the magical moment when the sun paints the sky with magical hues of orange and pink. As you ascend, you'll pass through diverse landscapes, from lush forests to volcanic rocks, creating a thrilling and ever-changing journey.

Reaching the top of Mount Batur is incredibly rewarding. You'll be treated to awe-inspiring panoramic views of Lake Batur and the surrounding countryside from the summit. It's a sight that will leave you in awe of Bali's natural beauty.

The trek itself is moderately challenging, but with the help of experienced guides, you'll be able to navigate the trail safely. Along the way, you'll learn about the geological significance of the volcano and its cultural importance to the Balinese people.

Overall, the Mount Batur trek is an unforgettable adventure that combines stunning natural scenery, physical activity, and a sense of accomplishment. It's an experience that will stay with you long after you've returned home.

## Bali Swing and Jungle

The Bali Swing is a thrilling attraction that allows you to swing high above the jungles. It's a must-visit for adventure seekers and those looking for a unique and exhilarating experience. As you soar through the air on the swing, you'll feel a rush of adrenaline.

But the Bali Swing is not just about swinging. It's also an opportunity to immerse yourself in the beauty of the jungle. The greenery, towering trees, and exotic wildlife create a vibrant atmosphere that transports you to another world. You can explore the jungle on foot, taking in the sights and sounds of nature, or even try other activities like zip-lining or trekking.

The Bali Swing and Jungle experience is about adventure, connecting with nature, and finding peace in the serene surroundings. So, if you're looking for an unforgettable adventure and a chance to experience the beauty of Bali's jungles, the Bali Swing and Jungle is the perfect choice.

## Bali Bird Park and Zoo

The Bali Bird Park and Zoo is a nature and animal lovers' paradise. It's a place where you can get up close and personal with a wide variety of beautiful birds and fascinating animals. The park is home to over 1,000 birds of different species, including rare and endangered ones. You can witness their rich colors, listen to their melodious songs, and even have the chance to feed and interact with some of them.

But the Bali Bird Park and Zoo is not just about birds. It's also a sanctuary for other animals, such as orangutans, crocodiles, and even Komodo dragons. You can learn about their habitats, behaviors, and conservation efforts to protect these incredible creatures.

Exploring the park is like embarking on a journey through different ecosystems. You'll walk through lush gardens, tropical rainforests, and even a walk-in aviary where you can feel like you're part of the bird's world. Moreover, the park offers educational shows and presentations where you can learn more about the animals and their natural habitats.

The Bali Bird Park and Zoo is a must-visit destination. It's a place where you can connect with nature, appreciate the beauty of wildlife, and create unforgettable memories.

## Key Takeaways

Opposing popular opinions, Bali has a bunch of fun activities to take part in apart from just sightseeing.

The zoo, jungle, and Mount Batur Trek are excellent places to visit for the adventure of a lifetime.

# CHAPTER 10

# Island Cuisine

Let's walk you through a flavorful journey through Bali's culinary scenery. From unique spice pastes to tantalizing dishes and fun cooking classes, you will learn all about the diverse and ethnic flavors of the fascinating province by reading this chapter.

**Balinese Flavors**

Sightseeing historical and religious landmarks in Bali may be at the top of your travel bucket list. However, to further enrich your enthralling experience on the island, you must try Balinese cuisine, for the mixture of two traditional spice pastes—*base genep* and *base gede* are the cornerstones of their food spectrum.

Tasting their delectable dishes will not only bring you closer to the Balinese culture but may also reveal that your palate leans toward the exotic richness dominating their cuisine while allowing you to understand the hype for their piquant flavors (Exquisite & Media, 2020).

What also sets Balinese cuisine apart from Indonesian cuisine is the Hindu population that predominates the island, making dishes with pork available that you might not find elsewhere in the country. This is, hence, another reason why tourists incessantly rave about the province's local cuisine.

**Must-Try Dishes**

Further diving into the island's resonant cultural heritage, here are five tantalizing dishes you must explore during your trip. You can find these dishes in renowned restaurants and street food vendors.

1. *Nasi Campur Bali* is a classic Indonesian dish. The delightful blend of traditional flavors makes it unique to Bali. Restaurants serve the staple dish with steamed rice and side dishes like *sate, tempe,* shredded chicken, samba, and bean sprouts. Each restaurant serves it their way, making it a new tasting experience for you each time you have it.
2. *Babi Guling* is an Indonesian term that translates to *turning pig,* and it is a signature Balinese dish exclusive to the island, as other regions of Muslim-majority Indonesia do not typically serve it. It is a celebratory dish that was once traditionally presented at important religious ceremonies. But as the island became a popular tourist destination, it is now served widely in several Balinese restaurants. To prepare Babi Guling, chefs will marinate the pig in spices such as shallots, lemongrass, coriander, and turmeric and slowly roast it on a rolling spit above an open fire with wood or coconut husks as fuel. They will serve it with a plate of steamed rice, pork crackling, fresh vegetables, and popular Balinese side dishes like *lawar.*
3. *Tum Ayam* is a side dish that entices the taste buds of most tourists, and it will do the same for yours. It is a flavorful blend of finely minced chicken enriched with spices and herbs. It is then wrapped in banana leaves, stitched on one end, and either steamed or grilled, depending on your preference, until the flavors saturate the dish (Macatulad, 2022).
4. *Lawar*, although often complementary to Babi Guling, can also be devoured as a dish on its own. It is a unique combination of crisp vegetables, shredded coconut, ground meat, and a blend of an array of aromatic herbs and spices, which Balinese cuisine is well-known for. Furthermore, the dish sometimes includes fresh blood. What makes it more unique is that each village throughout the island has its distinct variation.

5. *Bebek Betutu* is another ceremonial dish, which translates to slow-cooked duck. Bebek Betutu is such a revered dish that chefs cook it a day earlier. The duck has to be massaged with tamarind puree and salt to eliminate the distinctive odors of the duck and make the meat more tender. After washing it, the cook will stuff eggs, *bumbu rajeng*, and cassava leaves, a mixture of spices for the dish. After wrapping the duck in betel nut busks and *upeh*, chefs leave it to cook slowly until the meat becomes so tender that it easily separates from the bone (Brown, 2015).

## Cooking Classes

There is no doubt that you will miss these rich and aromatic herbs and spice-infused flavors once the duration of your trip ends.

But the good news is that Bali offers plenty of opportunities for you to learn how to cook its palatable dishes, explore its cuisine, visit local markets, and form a deeper connection with locals and other tourists. So when you return home, you will carry a tinge of these Balinese tastes with you.

Cooking classes in Bali will let you cook several of these traditional dishes and taste the food once the course ends, which can be quite rewarding and fulfilling. The classes are typically priced between $20 and $32, letting you cook about 5–10 dishes in half a day.

Here are three top-rated cooking classes that you can join in Bali (Tryon, 2023):

1. *Subak Cooking Class* is 15 km North of Ubud, which lets you make 9 dishes in 5 hours for $20. They will welcome you with a drink, paddy, and market tour, teach you recipes, and even offer a pick-and-drop service in the Ubud area.
2. *Ketut's Cooking Class Bali* is 3 km Northeast of Ubud, which will let you cook and taste 8 dishes in 4 hours for $25. They also include a pick-and-drop service in their package with a tour around the marketplace.

3. *Paon Bali Cooking Class* is 3 km East of Ubud. The course will teach you how to cook 7 dishes inside a traditional Balinese house. It is a 5-hour class that will cost you $25, including a market tour for morning classes, a Bintang beer with food, and a free hotel transfer from Ubud.

**The Island's Most Popular Restaurants**

Finding the perfect restaurant to try local Balinese cuisine could be tricky as many international restaurants serving European food have opened up after the island became a popular tourist attraction.

But don't fret because I have curated a list of the best renowned mouth-watering *warungs*—small Indonesian restaurants—in Bali:

*Clear Cafe* is a restaurant in Ubud, the perfect hotspot for vegans, vegetarians, and those of you who prioritize health and fitness. They operate all week from 8 a.m.–11 p.m. The average pricing is $3.30–$5 per entree. *Address:* Jl. Hanoman No. 8, Ubud, Kecamatan Ubud, Kabupaten Gianyar, Bali 80571, Indonesia.

*Pak Malen* is the place to go to taste the classic Babi Guling dish that every local and tourist rave about. It is a favorite spot for many tourists, so you might have to wait if you visit during peak hours. However, they operate every day of the week from 8:30 a.m.–7 p.m. You must expect to pay around $3 per Babi Guling. *Address:* Jalan Sunset Road No. 554, Seminyak, Kuta, Seminyak, Kuta, Kabupaten Badung, Bali 80361, Indonesia.

*Naughty Nuri* is an iconic warung that now has several branches in Bali, one in Jakarta, and some in Phuket, Kuala Lumpur, Melbourne, and Macau for international food lovers. However, nothing beats the local branch in Bali, where the delectable ribs and martinis are well-adored. They operate daily from 11 a.m.–10 p.m., and you can expect to pay $10 for the pork ribs and $8.20 for the martinis (Macatulad, 2019). *Address:* Jalan Mertanadi No. 62 Kerobokan Seminyak, Kerobokan Kelod, Kec. Kuta Utara, Kabupaten Badung, Bali 80361, Indonesia.

*Warung Makan Bu Rus* is a humble Balinese restaurant known best for their *Nasi Campur* dish, which costs around $3.20. It operates daily from 10:30 a.m.–10 p.m. *Address:* Jalan Suweta No. 9, Ubud, Kecamatan Ubud, Kabupaten Gianyar, Bali 80571.

*Menega Cafe* is the best hotspot for seafood lovers, right by Jimbaran Beach, where you can fill up your stomach while viewing the dazzling sunset. It operates every day from 11 a.m.–9.30 p.m. (Michelle, 2023). *Address:* 6597+MR6, Jalan Four Seasons Muaya Beach, Jimbaran, Kabupaten Badung, Bali 80361.

**Key Takeaways**

Balinese cuisine is recognized by a flavorful blend of spice pastes, *base gede*, and *base genep*, creating tangy flavors.

Due to the Hindu majority populating the province, most dishes with pork are widely available there, distinguishing it from other Indonesian cuisines.

Bali offers an array of must-try dishes, including Babi Guling, Nasi Campur Bali, Tum Ayam, Bebek Betutu, and Lawar.

It also provides affordable cooking classes, ranging from $20–$32, allowing tourists to learn and taste ethnic Balinese flavors.

Renowned *warungs* like Naughty Nuri, Clear Cafe, Pak Melen, Menega Cafe, and Warung Makan Bu Rus offer authentic Balinese cuisine.

These dining options offer a plethora of options, ranging from seafood delights and vegan options, providing a diverse culinary experience.

CHAPTER 11

# Wellness and Relaxation

Diving into Bali's world-renowned fitness and wellness culture, learning about Balinese spa traditions, wellness centers and resorts, and yoga and meditation spots in fantasy-like settings, I'll tell you lots about wellness and relaxation spots in Bali.

**Balinese Spa Traditions**

People appreciate Balinese spa treatments worldwide, for they are a significant part of the wellness culture of the province. They provide the perfect relaxation retreat after a long year. Taking a day off to get a Balinese spa treatment is essential for winding down and relaxing. Bali offers many kinds of spa treatments, ranging from luxury options to budget-friendly choices. Prices start at around $6 per hour for an entire body massage, making high-quality massages affordable.

Balinese spa treatments are recognized for their healing herbs, various massage techniques, aromatherapy, hot stone therapy, and facial masks using herbal pastes.

The spa treatment finds its roots in *esotericism*, "a belief that harmony lurks between the soul and the body." This traditional massage therapy comprises conventional massage, aromatherapy, and acupuncture. It focuses on lymphatic drainage, getting rid of muscle knots, and working on regulating blood circulation, which in turn will leave you stress-free and completely relaxed.

This fusion of massage techniques with a coconut and turmeric body scrub with a rice mask will leave your body feeling nourished and tranquil. Some spas even include bathtubs with rose leaves (*Surf Vacations and Balinese Spa*, 2017). On the island known as The Island of the Gods, floral baths are adored by many those who seek spa treatment.

While lying with your face down, your therapist will make use of reflexology to activate pressure points in your feet and work their way up to massage the deep tissues in your lower limbs, your thighs, and then your spinal area to enhance blood circulation and relieve tension in your shoulder muscles.

After that, when you lie on your back, the therapist will repeat the procedure by massaging your stomach to improve reproductive and digestive health. Some Balinese spas even include forehead and scalp massages.

Aromatherapy is the centerpiece of a Balinese massage treatment. Scents native to the island, such as frangipani, jasmine, lemongrass, and coconut, have been used by conventional healers for centuries and continue to be an integral component of authentic Balinese spa treatment (*It's Me-Time*, 2019).

**Wellness Centers**

Many cherish Bali's immersive wellness retreats, and so will you once you visit them. The island offers many places for working on your physical, mental, and spiritual well-being (SHEPPARD, 2022):

1. *COMO Shambhala Estate* is a gorgeous luxury jungle retreat surrounded by rice terraces and green fields, painting an exotic dreamlike scene. The place is perfect for engaging in physical activities and working toward your fitness goals. The package incorporates wellness activities, including fitness, spa, meals, and a personal butler.
2. *REVĪVŌ Wellness Resort* is a wellness resort in the Nusa Dua district designed to help you leave the pressures of life behind, featuring a sunken tub, pool, garden, courtyard, spa, and a salt flotation therapy session.
3. *Fivelements* excelled in traditional wellness, receiving an award for being an eco-haven in Bali's Ubud region. The

place is renowned for its fusion of Balinese healing traditions and modern holistic approaches. Their iconic retreats offer nutritious meals, lodging, wellness consultations, massages, and Balinese ceremonies. It also includes energy sessions, yoga, meditation classes, and water healing.
4. *COMO Uma Canggu* lies near Seminyak, a beachfront resort with Bali's finest surf break. TropicSurf partners with them, allowing surfing experiences suitable for all levels, including family programs. The resort features holistic therapies, Pilates, daily fitness classes, and *COMO Shambhala* wellness cuisine. It is a tranquil alternative to Kuta and Seminyak's crowded beach club scene.

**Yoga and Meditation**

Where most individuals prefer air-conditioned rooms for yoga to be relaxing, meditating in the open air around Mother Nature is the ultimate healing experience you could ever wish for. Yoga *shalas* and wellness centers are prevalent throughout the province due to its Buddhist and Hindu spiritual history.

Azadi Retreat in Ubud is the perfect open-air yoga *shala* if you want to meditate with the picturesque scenery around you. You can also see Mount Agung in the background, all under $57.07.

Om Ham Retreat & Resort is the optimal luxury place set at an affordable price of $340 that will offer you a breathtaking view of bountiful foliage and rice fields, along with a private pool and gardens. Now that's a place ideal for meditation and yoga.

Serenity Yoga Lembongan has a mesmerizing beachfront that requires you to take a boat ride from Sanur to get there, an excellent spot for introverted individuals of all levels who prefer to learn and practice yoga away from the crowds. You only have to pay around $52 for 4 days and 3 nights (Swagachi, 2021).

## Key Takeaways

Bali offers plenty of treatments focusing on various preferences and budgets, with prices starting from only $6 per hour, making high-quality spa treatments affordable.

Balinese spas combine healing herbs, acupuncture, aromatherapy, herbal pastes, diverse massage techniques, and facial masks to ensure a holistic and relaxing experience.

Bali features luxurious retreats like REVĪVŌ Wellness Resort and COMO Shambhala Estate, where they offer extravagant spa treatments and personalized services.

Bali is excellent at merging tradition with modernity. Fivelements stands out for its quality, where the center incorporates ethnic Balinese healing techniques with modern holistic approaches, making guests' experience of wellness comprehensive and exquisite.

Azadi Retreat in Ubud offers open-air yoga and meditation in the middle of breathtaking natural scenery, including a phenomenal view of Mount Agung.

Om Ham Retreat & Resort is the luxury alternative for yogis, with lush gardens and private pools. Serenity Yoga Lembongan is the more affordable option, with a captivating beachfront view.

# CHAPTER 12

# Shopping and Souvenirs

In this chapter, we will uncover Bali's retail treasures by delving into ethnic markets offering unique cultural experiences, cheap artisanal crafts and souvenirs representing Javanese and Hindu tales, and modern shopping destinations meeting everyday needs (Move, 2022).

**Traditional Markets**

While Bali boasts modern shopping centers and endless lines of alluring shops, traditional markets on the island retain a unique appeal. These markets also cater as ideal hotspots for tourists to meet their daily needs and souvenir options.

The island is fortunate with such a vibrant culture, rich in art and fresh produce, and the credit goes to the green farmlands, artisans, local artists, and the ocean.

The Sunday market in Samadi Bali in Canggu is the perfect stop for you, especially if you are a yoga enthusiast. You will find yourself in the crowds of locals and expats expertly browsing through fresh produce and artisan goods. The local market offers a variety of goods such as chicken, fish, vegetables, goat cheese, and even homemade organic cosmetics.

The night market near Sanur's Sindhu Beach, known as Pasar Senggol, is a food lover's comfort spot. It's a bustling place with satay skewers, street food, and a wide range of traditional Javanese and Balinese dishes such as *martabak* and *gado-gado*. The market houses more than 300 stalls, drawing locals and travelers who enjoy browsing and savoring local cuisine. Additionally, it sells organic produce, groceries, and flowers for morning Balinese offerings.

Love Anchor, situated in trendy Canggy, stands out the most not just because of its prime Batu Bolong location, organic coffee, and vibrant *warungs* but also for its lively and energetic atmosphere accompanied by disco music, making it an irresistible spot to visit. Here, at the hub for independent-brand fashion, you can buy unique traditional vests, stylish sunglasses, and exquisite jewelry (*Local Markets in Bali*, 2022).

**Artisanal Crafts**

Aside from the wellness resorts, rugged mountains, cerulean ocean, and scenic places, people revere Bali for its art. It started as adornments for religious statues and temples, and then the Balinese adapted their art to cater to modern-day commercial needs.

Every village in Bali specializes in an art category—woodcarvers live in Ubud, working in their own studios and making painted creations. These crafts are passed down through generations, resulting in the sustainable preservation of their art.

Artisans craft Balinese carvings from stone or wood, representing tales derived from Hindu and Javanese culture. These masterful art pieces represent sacred deities, dancers, horses, and expressive faces while maintaining their traditional artistic elements.

You can find these skilled handcrafted carvings in many shops throughout the island, including colorful paintings of flowers, ceramic tiles, and even carvings dedicated to mask dance or barong, serving as ideal souvenirs you can take back home.

Bali *sarong* is another artisanal craft that many tourists adore, "a tye-dyed light fabric worn by visitors." The well-loved material ranges from Balinese batik designs and beach sarongs to the rarest kinds of textiles. You can find the most precious and expensive double ikat fabric from Tenganan, a village on the island, which women weave in a year due to its intricate and detailed embroidery (*5 Unique Bali Creations*, n.d.).

**Modern Shopping**

Because Bali has transitioned into a tourist hub, many vibrant boutiques, markets, and malls have been established alongside ethnic stores, where you can find everything ranging from designer products to traditional artisanship.

Here are some favorite spots you can indulge in retail therapy (Carissa, 2023):

1. *Seminyak Village* is a boutique shopping mall with everyday essentials from accessories to lifestyle brands and fashion available. You can find both local Balinese designs and cosmopolitan options. Several casual cafes and dining options line the mall.

2. *Bintang Shopping Center*—supermarket—is the largest economical shopping center, perfect for your budget-friendly trip. The market is in the center of Jalan Raya Seminyak, where you can find essentials for your trip, from mosquito repellents to household goods and souvenirs.
3. *Seminyak Kayu Aya Shopping Street* is a tourist favorite, established in the heart of the region, offering several dining and upscale shopping options—including home decor markets and art galleries.
4. *Kuta Square* is in the center of Kuta, an open-air shopping center with a blend of budget-friendly markets and high-end retailers that offer everything from fashion products to electronic devices. At the North end of the place, you can find fast food shops, jewelers, surf shops, and fashion boutiques.

**Key Takeaways**

The traditional markets in Bali offer authentic experiences and fulfill daily necessities. Sunday Markets in Samandi Bali and Pasar Senggol near Sanur's Sindhu Beach provide local organic produce and Balinese artisanal goods.

The Night Market and other markets serve as a paradise for food lovers, offering traditional Balinese and Javanese dishes and street food.

Balinese artists specialize in stone and wood carvings and painting stories from Javanese and Hindu cultures that souvenirs often reflect.

Handmade paintings, Bali sarongs, and carvings are a nod to Bali's rich cultural heritage.

The island offers many modern shopping options, ranging from malls to boutiques like Seminyak Village to more affordable options like the Bintang Shopping Center.

Marketplaces like Seminyak Kayu Aya Shopping Street and Kuta Square are perfect for retail therapy, offering upscale shopping, eateries, and entertainment.

# CHAPTER 13

# Family-Friendly Fun

In this chapter, you will learn about thrilling and fascinating family-friendly adventures to further enhance the beauty of your trip. From tourist gems nestled in the eastern reaches of the island to exotic animals, captivating animal shows, feeding piranhas and elephants with a tropical backdrop, and renowned eco-conscious waterparks with exhilarating slides, I have it all covered for you.

**Bali Safari Marine Park**

Aside from the scenic grandeur that adorns the island, Bali offers several recreational activities, with Bali Safari Marine Park being a local and tourist gem.

It will take approximately 1–1.5 hours to get to the park, located in the East of Bali, from Seminyak. There is also a market nearby where you can taste the biggest burger on the island.

The timings differ according to the type of ticket you purchase; for daytime safari, the park operates from 9 a.m.–5 p.m., and for nighttime safari, the timings are from 6 p.m.–10 p.m. The prices vary but mostly start from around $40–$76.

The park will first let you visit the aquarium and then take you to feed piranhas, but that only comes with daytime tickets. It will cost you $4.50 for 2 baits. The park has several other activities that you can enjoy, such as the animal show, elephant show, big cat show, Bali agung show, and then, of course, the safari trip. You can even stroll around the park and take in the fascinating ambiance of the place.

The safari is the most exciting part of the park, where you will drive around the place with many animals roaming around in their own designated territory. They have hippos eating in the water, rhinos, elephants, and even big cats.

After that, you can sate your appetite by visiting the Uma restaurant, where there's even a playground for children. The layout of the place is like that of a food court, where you can have a variety of dishes from Nisa Campur to *Pizza Rendang*, fries, and salads (*Bali Safari park review*, 2022).

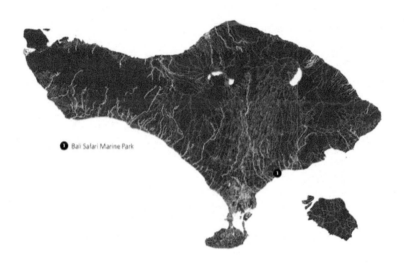

## Waterbom Bali

This place is not your ordinary escapade.

Ranked Asia's best waterpark, Waterbom Bali is a must-visit destination to cool off from the magical island's humid and warm climate.

The park is in an easily accessible region from Jimbaran and Seminyak in Kuta. Prices start at $34 for adults and $24 for children between 2 and 11 years of age and are free of cost for infants.

The park is a serene nature haven, with over half of the place covered in greenery and lush gardens. You can find fresh food—even baked goods—and handmade ice cream.

The best part is that the park prioritizes the environment by placing measures to reduce waste prediction, energy, and water use, earning the certification for being carbon neutral.

The park has seven extreme-level slides, with the biggest one being the most popular. Python, Constrictor, Twin Races, and Fast N Fierce are the more family-friendly options.

If you're looking for a little adrenaline rush, you must go through the Double Twist and Smashdown 2.0 rides.

The park can entertain children for hours with its water cannons, wheels, ropes, giant dump buckets, and slides. It has everything for everyone—gazebos, sun loungers, and chill areas like Fantastic and Lazy River.

If you are faint of heart, do not fret because every ride has a label mentioning the speed, thrill, and drench rating, allowing you to pick the best ride according to your preferences (Pauly, 2020).

**Elephant Safari Park**

Bali has several recreational sites for you to view overwhelming wildlife. However, the island has plenty of places to offer if you want to feel, wash, feed, and ride elephants in verdant tropical gardens *(Mason Elephant Park*, n.d.).

One high-ranked destination is Elephant Safari Park, located North of Ubud. Home to the rare and native breed of Sumatran Elephants, the park lets you breathe in the same air as them. The tropical rainforest surrounds the park, accentuating the beauty of Mother Nature and immersing you entirely as though you are out in the wild (Gurnani, 2021).

Mason Elephant Park is another well-loved site located in Ubud, where you can not only play, feed, wash, and ride elephants in their tropical habitat but also walk through well-maintained botanical gardens, stone carvings made by local artisans, and koi ponds. The tour guides will educate you on the elephant and even see elephants paint amid all other activities.

The park even has a mini-museum where you can view replicas of the skeletons of wooly mammoths and pristine artifacts such as Balinese Kris daggers and ancient carved tusks from other Indonesian islands (Intan, 2023).

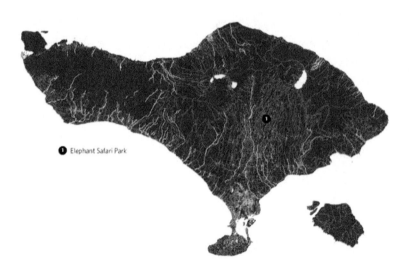

**Key Takeaways**

Bali Safari Marine Park is the perfect place for a family-friendly retreat, allowing animal interaction, the chance to feed them, and watch captivating shows.

Visitors can explore the park's diverse wildlife on a safari trip, with animals like rhinos, elephants, big cats, and hippos in their natural habitats.

Waterbom Bali offers a refreshing and rejuvenating retreat from the island's tropical climate with a variety of thrilling slides and family-friendly ventures.

The park is eco-conscious, prioritizing the environment and sustainability over everything, earning carbon-neutral certification. It also offers a verdant landscape with plenty of eateries.

Elephant Safari Park in North Ubud allows tourists to wash, ride, and feed native Sumatran elephants in a tropical rainforest setting.

Tourists can walk through well-kept botanical gardens and koi ponds while learning about ancient artifacts and wooly mammoths by visiting the mini-museum in the park.

CHAPTER 14

# Nightlife and Entertainment

This chapter covers a brief insight into the nightlife you can experience along with the entertainment it serves as you take a moment to relax and let go in the bars and pubs. Seminyak and Legian are the epicenter of nightlife, with bars and clubs that line the streets along the beach.

**Seminyak's Chic Bars and Clubs**

To say that Bali can be defined as a party place would not be far from the truth. Bars and clubs are a popular attraction among tourists in Bali. Whether you are a solo traveler or a couple looking for a break, Seminyak's beach side is lined with chic bars and clubs. The streets that come alive at night and the extremely welcoming people make it an even better experience.

If you're looking for unlimited fun in a crowded place, a perfect spot to start would be the Bali Joe Bar. With the perfect vibe, drag shows, and amazing staff—not to forget that it's a gay bar!—it is the most highly-rated bar in Seminyak. It makes for the best beginning to your night, full of memories.

Right in the heart of Seminyak is one of the more popular spots, Motel Mexicola. This vibrant and colorful venue encapsulates the essence of a Mexican fiesta, inviting visitors to indulge in a fiesta of flavors, music, and aesthetics. From its lively interiors adorned with traditional Mexican décor to its energetic atmosphere, Motel Mexicola offers an immersive experience. Feast on delectable Mexican cuisine, sip on margaritas, and enjoy the Latin music, creating unforgettable memories of Bali with a Mexican twist. Whether you're a food enthusiast, a partygoer, or someone seeking a unique cultural fusion, Motel Mexicola is a must-visit spot to add a splash of Latin American fiesta to your Bali experience.

One thing about Seminyak is the absolutely magnificent beachfront. If your goal also includes a place for good photos and scenery with a somewhat low-key vibe, Ku De Ta Bali should be your choice. A chic, sophisticated place with private lounges, cozy corners, and an exclusive bar makes Ku De Ta Bali one of the most well-known party hotspots. It overlooks the beach with its main lawn consisting of daybeds to relax in (*Ku de Ta Bali - Upscale Beachside*, 2023).

Right on Petitenget Street, Seminyak, you'll find the chic Mirror Bali Lounge and Club. With its gothic style interior and glittery wall decor, the modern laser and disco lights give an amazing party vibe. Similar to the gothic interior, if your interest is in a somewhat horror-themed place, Frankenstein's Laboratory has great offers. After all, who doesn't want to experience Halloween throughout the year? (*29 Best Nightlife in Seminyak*, 2023).

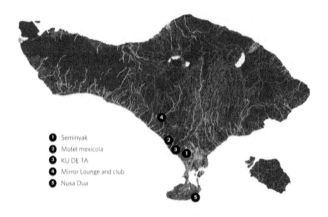

## Legian Street: Pub Crawls and Live Music

The vast variety of beach clubs, nightclubs, dinner cruises, and rooftop bars is endless. While going to a bar or club is a great way to spend your night, no one can resist bar hopping or pub crawling. It contains fun of its own, giving the thrill of exploration as well.

Legian Street not only connects Kuta to Seminyak but also pulls in all tourists and locals to its nightlife entertainment. It is the most crowded as a nighttime hub. It's multiple bars with live musical performances that regularly include not only local bands but international ones as well are the peak feature. Just think of how many live performances you can watch while going from one pub to another, hands full of cocktails and drinks, swaying to the music. And not only that! Sampling the savory street foods from street vendors in between is another plus point to this amazing experience.

From DJ battles and drag shows to live performances and Rasa Sayang parties, these bars are the best way to spend the night. And for this, The Bounty Bar is the finest example (Travioor, 2017).

If you feel like starting your nightlife entertainment early, the best opening to your bar-hopping experience would be Engine Room. It's a three-story nightclub that opens in the afternoon, earlier than all other clubs and pubs. Not only is the place amazing for partying but there's also a pool table where you can challenge others to a game! (*11 Best Nightlife Experiences in Legian*, 2023).

## Balinese Dance Performances

The Balinese dance performances range from modern theatrical dances to traditional dances performed in temples. They are beautifully choreographed dance pieces made exceptional with dramatic sound effects and lighting with an ostentatious display. The dances take you through heartfelt and intense storylines. Paired with colorful costumes, the dance troupes become the best storytellers.

Just to name a few of the Balinese traditional dances, there are the Barong dance, Jegog dance, Kacak dance, Topeng dance, etc. It can be said without a doubt that Balinese dances bring people closer to the culture and history of the nation, as well as the religion. These phenomenal dances are believed to be a way to connect with the gods.

If you wish to learn about the dances more in-depth, dance classes are available in the traditional Balinese villages—where you can also connect with the natives and learn about their lifestyle—or in private villas by professionals. Moreover, these graceful dances are a means to relax your body and be active at the same time—with all your body parts involved in the moves. The dances are the ultimate way to connect with not just your surroundings but also your inner self.

The Bali Agung theatrical show and Kecak at Uluwatu Temple Amphitheatre are two of the many popular dance performances you can watch while visiting the theaters *(14 Best Traditional Dance Shows*, 2021).

**Balinese Beach Clubs**

Potato Head Beach Club (Seminyak)

One of Bali's prized jewels, Potato Head Beach Club sits on the Seminyak shoreline. Known for its characteristic architecture and a mammoth infinity pool that seemingly tips into the Indian Ocean, this beach club is beachfront luxury. As the sun dips below the horizon, the atmosphere at Potato Head transforms into a dynamic nightlife hub. Live music, DJs, and signature cocktails make this spot a must-visit for partygoer.

Finns Beach Club (Canggu)

Nestled on the vibrant coastline of Canggu, Finns Beach Club epitomizes the Bali beach party spirit. One of the more famous Bali Beach clubs, it overlooks the famous Berawa Beach, it boasts a sun-soaked pool, an inviting bar, and multiple dining options. Surrounded by swaying palm trees and the rhythmic sounds of waves, Finns offers a laid-back yet upbeat vibe. Sunset sessions here are a true spectacle, with the sky ablaze in a bright palette, setting the scene for an exhilarating night ahead.

## Mrs. Sippy (Seminyak)

Mrs. Sippy, with its sprawling saltwater pool and high-dive platform, stands as a prominent name in Bali's beach club scene. Located in Seminyak, this tropical playground beckons visitors with its cool aura and Mediterranean-inspired architecture. It's a magnet for those seeking poolside relaxation, delectable cuisine, and exciting parties. With regular DJ performances and special events, Mrs. Sippy guarantees an unforgettable Bali experience.

## La Brisa (Canggu)

Inspired by the bohemian surf culture of Canggu, La Brisa is a rustic beachfront spot that seamlessly blends the island's natural beauty with sustainable design. Constructed from reclaimed wood and whimsical decor, it exudes a cozy and laid-back charm. With its beachfront swings, bamboo seating, and delicious seafood, La Brisa provides a perfect setting to unwind, dine, and revel in the ocean breeze.

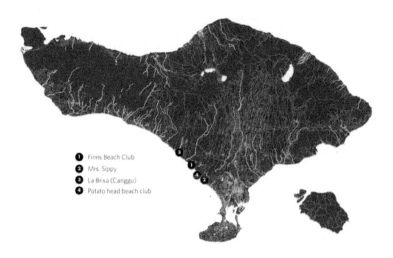

## Key Takeaways

The best nightlife to look for is in Seminyak. Bali Joe Bar is the perfect start to a night, especially with a group of friends or even as a solo traveler.

Ku De Ta is a chic and sophisticated place with a dedicated bar and restaurant, along with cozy corners and a beachfront that gives the best view of the sunset.

Bar hopping in Legian is the best way to spend your night while enjoying street foods.

The live musical performances only enhance the experience with DJ battles and even Rasa Sayang parties.

You haven't experienced the full Balinese culture and heritage if you haven't seen one of the traditional dances at one of the theaters.

Bali has an array of beach clubs to choose from

There are varieties of different dances, from old to modern.

Dance classes are available all over if anyone is interested. You can learn from a professional or even in a rural area with the locals while understanding more about their lifestyle, too.

# CHAPTER 15

# Beyond Bali—Day Trips and Island-Hopping

In this chapter, I will take you through the islands of Bali, Indonesia. It wouldn't be a lie when I say everything in Bali is in one place, and the islands are in another. Their beauty is too much for words, and marine life is a spectacle. Being on them is like being in paradise. And what's better than touring not one but many?

**Nusa Penida: Crystal Bays and Kelingking Beach**

While it is true that Bali is known for many things, its majestic islands are not so far behind. If you're not hopping from one island to another, then you're missing out a lot. The pure white sand and clear crystal water make the view all the more amazing. Additionally, swimming with the stingrays is not something you can do every day, so why not avail this opportunity?

In the Southeastern part of Bali, we find Nusa Penida. After a crazy day of partying and dance shows, it is the perfect place to relax. Moreover, Crystal Bay is a great spot if you love diving and snorkeling. Seeing the breathtaking coral reefs in the turquoise clear water is a once-in-a-lifetime opportunity. Furthermore, the great expanse of the island gives a perfect view of the sunset. A short distance from the beach are Broken Beach and Angel Billabong, and only about 40 minutes from Crystal Bay Beach is Kelingking Beach—you can even rent a motorbike or scooter to get there! (Teslaru, 2021).

With its T. rex shape, Kelingking Beach is a very popular spot. The unique topography only enhances the beauty of the view. Even better, it presents a good diving spot at the Manta Point, where you can swim with the manta rays!

## Lombok: Gili Islands and Mount Rinjani

During your island hopping, Lombok is a must-stop. The volcanic mountains, wondrous coral reefs, and fabulous waterfalls are only some additional perks to the beautiful beaches. Though there are several districts in Lombok, the major-practiced religion is Islam, making your visit even better because you can experience their lifestyle as well. Opening yourself to know more about another religion can never go wrong and only enhances the quality of your own life.

Another unique activity that can be found at Lombok is turtle conservation at Gili Island. Gili Island is now very touristy, but still not crowded. It makes for the perfect spot for a honeymoon as well. Gili Trawangan, Gili Air, and Gili Meno are the three most popular spots on Gili Island, with their crystal water, white sand, and relaxed vibes.

As for the volcanic mountains, Mount Rinjani is the most popular attraction. The stupendous mountain towers over Lombok, the second-highest peak in Indonesia. The stunning scenery and geological importance make it a tourist destination in Lombok, including the hot spring and huge crater lake where you can take a dip. Mount Rinjani National Park has visitors coming from all over to climb its summit, as well as roaming through the forests and viewing the magnificent waterfalls, embracing the splendor of nature. Mount Rinjani is indeed a gem of Indonesia (*Climbing Mount Rinjani*, 2018).

**Java: Borobudur and Prambanan Temples**

If you traveled to Indonesia but never went inside a single temple, it's safe to say you wasted a lot of your time. Java, a volcano-dotted island at the economic and geographical center of Indonesia, is known for its fantastic temples and picturesque landscapes. The island is so cheap and a perfect place for backpackers on a strict budget. The place has it all, so you can't feel like you missed out on something.

About 97.3% of Javanese are Muslim, and more than half the people live there, making it the most populated island in Indonesia.

The world's largest Buddhist temple, Borobudur Temple, is located in Central Java. Similarly, the largest Hindu temple in Indonesia, Prambanan Temple, is also in Java. The temples are a magnificent spectacle and tell the history of how the Buddhists and Hindus lived side-by-side in peace. The cultural and religious significance of these temples is immense. Additionally, the architectural importance of these temples—especially Borobudur Temple—cannot be missed. It would not come as a shock that Borobudur Temple Compounds is one of the Seven Wonders of the World (Milijana, 2019).

**Key Takeaways**

The best way to describe this magnificent place is by its white sand beaches and crystal-clear water.

Crystal Bay and Kelingking Beach are 2 places located within 40 minutes of each other that offer diving, snorkeling, and swimming with manta rays!

If you're feeling adventurous, head to Mount Rinjani. The volcanic mountain can be climbed to the summit. Moreover, the national park offers trips through the forests and to the waterfalls.

Gili Islands are perfect for honeymooners with a relaxed environment and not too much crowd.

If you're Muslim or looking forward to learning more about this religion, the Gili Islands are perfect for you.

A perfect place for backpacking and long trips with affordable side activities is Java. It is the most populated island in the country, with a Muslim majority.

Borobudur and Prambanan are the biggest Buddhist and Hindu temples, respectively. They are the perfect place to visit to learn more about the ancient Balinese heritage.

# CHAPTER 16

# Accommodation

The first thing to do while planning a trip is to look for suitable accommodation. This chapter will help you choose the perfect place to stay for the entirety of your trip to Bali.

**Types of Accommodation Options**

Some best places to choose for accommodation are Ubud, Kuta, Legian, Seminyak, Jimbaran, Canggu, etc. The several options in these areas can be villas, hotels, hostels, and even camping grounds.

Hostels: If you're looking for cheap accommodation, your best bet is the hostels all over Bali for a long-term stay.

Hotels: There is no lack of hotels in Bali. As one of the most popular and well-known tourist spots, the hotels range from cheap to expensive.

Villas: Small private villas in Bali offer intimacy and privacy for all.

Resorts: For a perfect five-star stay, you might have to settle for the resorts—especially if you're on a honeymoon!

Homestays: You can stay in family-owned hotels or bungalows close to the family (Tanja, 2022).

Guesthouses and Airbnbs: These are more affordable than hotels and resorts and offer a more authentic experience.

Eco lodges: Bali is known for its bamboo craftsmanship. Bamboo villas are the best example of experiencing authentic Balinese culture.

## Location Matters

While choosing a location for the perfect accommodation for yourself, you might need to consider what exactly attracts you the most. Whether you're looking for adventure or spirituality, lively nightlife, or a relaxing getaway, where you stay relies on it.

Ubud: If your main focus is the cultural heritage, Ubud is the place to go. The budget is from the mid to high range, and though the region is crowded in the central area, it is perfect. You can walk to temples and enjoy the laid-back environment with vegan food and coffee fields!

Canggu: Canggu is the most popular place if surfing and sunbathing on the beach attract you. It is best for its nightlife and is understandably the most expensive place in Bali.

Seminyak: Seminyak has a mid-range budget to live there, which proves excellent as it is affordable to many. It has a lively city atmosphere with a beachfront and fantastic nightlife. Moreover, the most affordable villas are located in Seminyak. It is perfect for those visiting for the first time.

Uluwatu and Bukit Peninsula: The most incredible coastal life is offered at Uluwatu and Bukit Peninsula. This is cheaper than Canggu and close to the airport with a spectacular ocean view and less crowds. It is the ideal place for ocean and water sports lovers.

Amed: It is a very less-known area of Bali that is perfect for explorers and people looking forward to knowing more about the traditional and authentic side of Bali. It is one of the cheapest places and is always less crowded because of the beaten track (Hair, 2023).

Sidemen: Right in the middle of some rice field terraces, Sidemen offers a magnificent view of the sacred Mount Agung. The extremely cheap and quiet area has the most welcoming locals. The rural feel gives an authentic Balinese vibe, which is best for nature lovers. The bamboo houses are a recommended accommodation.

Nusa Dua: Nusa Dua is a closed-off, perfect getaway for family gatherings at villas and honeymoon resorts. As one of the best spots for water sports, Nusa Dua is a favorite among people. The beautiful sunsets and amazing dive spots make a great background for pictures.

## Popular Hotels, Hostels, and Other Accommodation Types Across the Island

The accommodation is varied across the island. From $3 per night in a hostel to $300 in a luxurious villa, the options are endless.

Lushy Hostels: The wide range of hostels is located in Canggu. They provide great co-working spaces and air-conditioned rooms with indoor activities. Not to forget, Lushy Hostels are extremely affordable.

Bali Jungle Camping: For an elevated experience of camping, located within a remote coffee plantation, Bali Jungle Camping is an amazing accommodation. Surrounded by nature with dome tents and wooden cabins, it gives a private escape (*15 MOST UNIQUE PLACES*, 2022).

Hotel Tugu: One of the best hotels at Canggu Beach is Hotel Tugu, known for preserving cultural heritage. There are plenty of cafes and restaurants—even vegetarian!—that give the most relaxed vibe and atmosphere. It is also possible to live in dorms and private rooms.

Alila Seminyak: Alila Seminyak resort, located in downtown Seminyak, offers luxury and relaxation at the beachfront. The terraced rooms and suites are the perfect choice for you. There are outdoor swimming pools and spas in the resort as well.

## Key Takeaways

A vast variety of types of accommodation are present in Bali in every place, from cheap to expensive.

For long trips, hostels are highly recommended as they are the cheapest, while hotels and resorts work for shorter trips.

If you're a first-time traveler, your best bet would be Ubud or Canggu.

Uluwatu and Bukit Peninsula, along with Amed, are the quietest places if you're going for a relaxed vacation.

For water rafting and beautiful waterfalls, Sidemen is the place.

Seminyak is the peak attraction if you're interested in nightlife.

Cheap: Lushy Hostels are a very affordable place for you, especially for a long stay.

Calm: Bali Camping Ground is away from civilization and gives a relaxed environment surrounded by nature.

Cultural: Hotel Tugu preserves the culture like no other place and definitely brings you closer to the Balinese culture.

Luxury: Alila Seminyak is a luxurious resort in downtown Seminyak.

## CHAPTER 17

# Capturing Bali Through Photography

In this chapter, we will journey through Bali's most majestic locations, from the towering Sekumpul Waterfall to the legendary Handara Golf and Resort Bali Gates and the tranquil Tegalalang Rice Terrace. I have also touched on a crucial aspect you must consider on your trip: cultural sensitivity. This is to ensure that you travel with the utmost respect and embrace vibrant Balinese customs.

**Best Photo Spots**

Nothing can quite replicate the overwhelming feeling of being present at the moment, but if there's anything that comes close to it, it is reliving those moments through the pictures you take. Capture your moments on the ethereal island of Bali in these picturesque locations.

*Sekumpul Waterfall* is the tallest and mightiest of the many waterfalls in Bali. You will have to walk down a muddy road and then cross a river, but I can assure you that each step you take will be worth it for the breathtaking view of the waterfall as it cascades down to the base.

*Handara Golf & Resort Bali Gates* is the location you must visit for your travel photo collection. The irresistible grandeur of the tall elongated gates and the stunning verdant backdrop of the island is one you wouldn't want to miss. The crack of dawn is the best time to visit the location, where you only have to pay a dollar to take photos.

*Mount Batur* is another scenic location, perfect for early birds. A two-hour hike is required to get there before sunrise, but the view that will bless both your eyes and the camera lens will be worth waking up at 3 a.m (Pauly, 2023).

*Tegalalang Rice Terrace* is the most recognizable and visited spot in Bali. If you skip visiting the location, you have not really seen Bali. You wouldn't want to miss the amber rays that slip through palm trees and the stairs of Mother Nature. Tegalalang is in the center of Bali, near Ubud, and getting there is almost free, apart from the small donations that local farmers might request if you want to get there.

*Pura Ulun Danu Beratan Temple* is also known as the floating temple. It is a stunning Hindu Shaivite Shiva temple nestled on the shores of Lake Bratan. It earned the nickname, floating temple, due to the way rainwater collects around it, making it appear as something straight out of a picture book. The location is best appreciated in the early morning when the first glimmer of sunlight reflects off the lake surrounding it (Greta, 2020).

**Cultural Sensitivity**

As tourists, we must ensure that we proceed with sensitivity and respect when visiting the island to preserve its diversity while educating ourselves on the Balinese culture and religious customs. Abiding by the basic etiquette of the ancient island's culture will further enhance our experience and make the locals around us comfortable and even more hospitable and welcoming.

The first rule is to dress appropriately, especially when visiting sacred places such as Synagogues, Mosques, and Churches. You must be wearing a scarf around your waist or a sarong. Anything that falls below the knees works, too. Moreover, you must cover your midriff, chest, and shoulders while visiting these locations.

It is imperative that you follow the same rules when you stroll through villages, and it is best to avoid wearing revealing and skintight clothing unless you are at the beach (*Bali Respect*, n.d.).

Remember, gestures are an essential part of Balinese communication. Using your thumb as a gesture is best to avoid any misunderstandings, but never point your index finger at anything, as that is considered disrespectful. Touching the top of someone's head, especially a child's, is also an impolite gesture as it is considered a sacred body part.

Furthermore, ensuring you know basic table manners according to the Balinese culture is crucial as the locals consider eating with your left hand as unhygienic, preferring to follow the custom of eating with the right hand.

In addition, when paying money, it is customary to use both hands to show respect (Thalpe, 2023).

Knowing how to communicate politely is also an important thing to consider. The Balinese appreciate it when tourists speak softly with their voices low. The Balinese tend to avoid all sorts of confrontation; should you find yourself in a disagreement, it is best to make amends with the person involved.

Furthermore, the Balinese consider feet to be dirty. It is essential to take off your shoes before you walk into a sacred location or a house. It is also worth remembering to never point your feet at a person, especially someone older than you because that is considered quite disrespectful (*Adjusting to the Culture in Bali*, n.d.).

**Key Takeaways**

Bali is full of natural beauty. Popular captured gems include Handara Golf & Resort Bali Gates, Mount Batur, Sekumpul Waterfall, Tegalalang Rice Terrace, and Pura Ulun Danu Beratan Temple, encapsulating the island's enchanting landscapes.

Respecting local traditions when visiting sacred locations by wearing modest clothing is extremely important.

To dress modestly when visiting temples and villages is crucial. Avoid skin-tight and revealing clothing. It is best to wear a sarong and long shirts that fall below the knees and cover the shoulders.

Pointing with your index finger is considered impolite. The Balinese prioritize table manners, eating with the right hand, and using both hands when handing out money. They speak softly, avoid confrontation, and remove shoes before entering a sacred building or a house.

CHAPTER 18

# Safety and Health in Bali

This chapter covers all the essential aspects of safety and health during your vacation in Bali. Learn about the precautions, potential health risks, and vaccinations, along with staying vigilant against local hazards and common scams. Additionally, I have included crucial emergency contacts and medical facilities for your ease.

**Health Precautions and Vaccinations**

I advise you to consult a healthcare professional or a vaccination center at least six to eight weeks before your planned trip to Bali.

Bali is a developed region in comparison to other places in Indonesia. Hence, it is important to consider the various diseases that could potentially affect you during your time there.

A variety of viruses are contracted from insects, such as flies, ticks, and fleas. However, mosquitoes are the leading insects in spreading these illnesses.

Dengue fever is the most common viral infection in Bali, with the severity varying from mild to serious. It is best to wear insect-repellent and long-sleeved shirts and pants. Close your windows and doors to prevent mosquitoes from entering your residence, and use mosquito nets in outdoor areas.

Note that traveler's diarrhea, dubbed as Bali's belly, is relatively common and doesn't last for more than a couple of days. However, it is important to book a doctor's consultation if you face symptoms for over 48–72 hours. To prevent getting traveler's diarrhea, I recommend you only eat in restaurants and locations that practice good hygiene (*Bali*, n.d.).

Vaccinations that must be up-to-date before your flight to Bali include flu shots (influenza), polio, chickenpox, measles-mumps-rubella, shingles, and diphtheria-tetanus-pertussis. You must also make sure you have received all required COVID-19 vaccines. Healthcare professionals recommend medication for preventing malaria and vaccines for measles and yellow fever. Because rabid mammals and dogs are everywhere in Indonesia, especially in rural regions, you must avoid petting them unless you are sure they are completely vaccinated to prevent rabies (*Indonesia - Traveler View*, n.d.).

**Staying Safe: Common Scams and Local Hazard**

Like anywhere in the world, you may come across scammers in Bali. Recognizing them might be tricky at first, which is why it is important to always be vigilant during your trip.

If you want to commute around the island, take an authentic service such as Bluebird Taxis instead of regular ones to avoid drivers charging you unreasonable rates. Bluebird Taxis are light blue, with the logo of a bird on the side and the top of the car. Drivers wear blue-colored uniforms and use a meter with their identification labeled on the dashboard.

While some touring locations may be advertised as free, this can sometimes be a tactic to encourage tourists to make huge donations at the end of the tour.

Moreover, street vendors often pester tourists into buying or renting sarongs for ridiculous prices. It is best to bring your sarong.

At the beach, you may notice people coming up to you offering to do your hair, nails, massages, tattoos, buying bracelets, souvenirs, or sarongs. Oftentimes, these products and services are extremely overpriced; hence, I recommend you ignore their persuasion and find dedicated shops, tattoo places, or hair salons.

Another relatively common scam is money exchangers clandestinely dropping your money or reducing the actual amount you're supposed to get during money exchange. To avoid this, visit an authorized money changer, where they ensure the exchange rate is up-to-date. Also, count the amount that you get back to avoid any unnecessary scams (*20 Common Bali Scams*, 2023).

**Emergency Contacts and Medical Facilities**

You should always be prepared in the face of an emergency—whether it is medical or anything else. The reassuring news is that healthcare is significantly more affordable in Bali than in the West, with the majority of it accessible in touristy regions. Here are the contacts to accredited medical facilities in Bali (*Tourists in Bali?*, 2023):

*Tabanan General Hospital*—Rumah Sakit Umum Tabanan—*Contact*: +62 361 227 91, *Address*: Jl. Pahlawan, Delod Peken, Kec. Tabanan, Kabupaten, Tabanan, Bali

*BIMC Hospital, Contact*: +62 361 761 26, *Address*: Jl. By Pass Ngurah Rai No. 100X, Kuta, Badung, Bali

*Siloam Hospitals, Contact*: +62 361 779 900, *Address*: Jl. Sunset Road No. 818, Seminyak, Kuta, Badung, Bali

*Bali Royal Hospital, Contact*: +62 361 849 6646, *Address*: Jl. Mahendradatta No. 57, Denpasar, Bali.

In case of an emergency, here are some important contacts you must be aware of (*Bali Emergency Numbers*, n.d.):

1. Main emergency: 112
2. Ambulance: 118
3. Police: 110
4. Search and Rescue: 111, 115, and 151
5. Fire Department: 113

## Key Takeaways

Consult a healthcare provider at least a month and a half before leaving for Bali. Your vaccinations must be up-to-date, including polio, chickenpox, measles, COVID-19, etc.

Always apply insect repellents to prevent mosquito bites.

Always stay vigilant during your trip. Using reputable transportation like Bluebird Taxis with verified IDs is the best way to commute around the island. Avoid individuals offering *free* tours as they come with hidden costs.

Street vendors may unreasonably increase prices. Use authorized money exchangers and always count the received amount.

Bali has plenty of affordable and easily accessible local and international healthcare options with many facilities.

Always have emergency numbers ready. Remember 112 for main emergencies, 118 for ambulances, 110 for police, 111, 155, and 151 for Search and Rescue, and 113 for the Fire Department.

CHAPTER 19

# Balinese Language Tips

Communication is the essence of human interactions and the exchange of ideas, information, thoughts, and feelings, as without communication, the concept of human connectivity would collapse. Language is the foundational pillar for communication, and in this chapter, I will tell you all the necessary Balinese language phrases and insights through language that will make your travel as smooth as butter, particularly if you're a foreigner.

**Basic Phrases**

To get things started, I'm going to begin with fundamental phrases that one needs to know for introductory purposes, and then, slowly, the diversity of the introductory phrases will increase, giving you a deeper range of communication abilities.

"I", in Balinese, is *Tiyang* or *Cang*, and "You are" is *Ragane*. "What's your name?" is referred to as *Nyen Adan Ranane/CI?* "My name is": *Adan Tiyang/Cang,* and "How are you?": *Ken-ken kabare?* "I'm fine" in Balinese is *Tiyang/Cang becik-becik,* "Where are you from?" is *Uling dija ragane/ci,* and "I'm from" is *Tiyang/Cang uling.* "Thanks" is *Suksma,* and "You're welcome" is *Suksma Mewali.* "Yes" is called *Nggih* or *Inggih,* and "no" is *Nenten.* "Hi" in Balinese is *Hai* and "Hello" is *Halo.* "Good morning" is *Rahajeng semeng* and "Good afternoon" is *Rahajeng tengai* (Wayan, 2023).

Furthermore, in Balinese, the word *Gek* can refer to a lady or a young woman, and *Bil* can be used as a male or a brother. *Ibu* can be said to call a lady who is older, as in your mother's age, and *Pak* means mister and can be used to address anyone whose gender is male (Wayan, 2023).

## Insights Through Language

The Balinese language originated from the Austronesian language family, which falls under the Malayo-Polynesian language's banner. Around 3.3 million people speak this language, and the predominant areas include the Indonesian island of Bali, eastern Lombok, and northern Nusa Penida. The language of Balinese is still growing and not hugely popular because the younger generation has not adopted speaking Balinese entirely; therefore, the youth proficiency is low.

In Lampung Province, the Balinese language is almost instinctive because much facilitation is given to the language in that province, thus resulting in shallow Balinese exposure. The trans-migrants in the province mostly prefer to speak Indonesian and Javanese, which causes different languages to mix via code mixing and switching. Balinese is a support language because the natives form new words by combining Balinese and Indonesian root words and Javanese and Balinese affixes (Macrae, n.d.).

## Key Takeaways

In Balinese, the most essential phrases for introductory purposes are *Hai* for saying "Hello," *Nyen Adan Ranane/CI* for asking someone's name, and *Adan Tiyang/Cang* for telling your name.

"Thanks" is *Suksma*, and "You're welcome" is *Suksma Mewali*. "Yes" is called *Nggih* or *Inggih*, and "No" is *Nenten*.

Around 3.3 million people speak this language, and the predominant areas include the Indonesian island of Bali, eastern Lombok, and northern Nusa Penida.

Balinese is a support language because the natives form new words by combining Balinese and Indonesian root words and Javanese and Balinese affixes.

# 100 Tips to Consider

1. Check whether your country requires a visa for Bali.
2. Book your flight in advance to get cheaper airfare.
3. Have a valid passport of six months.
4. Make sure you have travel insurance due to Bali's activities.
5. Have a contact number handy in case of emergencies.
6. Choose the right time to visit the island.
7. Carry an insect repellant when you travel.
8. Pack summer clothes.
9. Pack a swimsuit and extra towels.
10. Explore the stunning rice terraces in Tegalalang.
11. Visit the iconic Uluwatu Temple and catch a traditional Kecak dance performance.
12. Experience a spiritual journey at Tirta Empul, a sacred water temple.
13. Take part in a traditional Balinese cooking class at places like Subak Cooking class and Nia Balinese Cooking Class. Learn to make local dishes.
14. Don't miss the chance to try authentic Balinese cuisine like Nasi Goreng and Babi Guling.
15. Rent a scooter to easily navigate through Bali's traffic and explore at your own pace.
16. Stay hydrated and drink plenty of water, especially in hot and humid weather.
17. Respect the local culture and traditions by dressing modestly when visiting temples.

18. Use sunscreen to protect your skin from the strong Bali sun.
19. Bargain when shopping at local markets to get the best prices as the locals will inflate the price if they can tell you are a tourist.
20. Take a surf lesson in one of Bali's famous surf spots like Kuta or Canggu.
21. Visit the Goa Gajah Temple, also known as the Elephant Cave.
22. Explore the vibrant street art scene in Bali's artistic hub, Ubud.
23. Attend a traditional Balinese dance performance to witness the rich cultural heritage.
24. Take a sunrise hike to the top of Mount Batur for breathtaking views.
25. Try snorkeling or diving in the crystal-clear waters of Menjangan Island.
26. Visit the Bali Safari and Marine Park for an unforgettable wildlife experience.
27. Learn about Balinese spirituality by attending a traditional ceremony or ritual.
28. Get a traditional Balinese massage to relax and rejuvenate.
29. Stay in a traditional Balinese homestay to experience the local way of life.
30. Visit Tegal Wangi Beach for stunning sunset views.
31. Explore the hidden waterfalls of Bali, like Tegenungan or Gitgit.
32. Take a yoga class in Ubud, known as the yoga capital of Bali.

33. Visit the famous Tanah Lot Temple and witness the beautiful sunset.

34. Learn to make traditional Balinese handicrafts like wood carvings or batik.

35. Explore the Monkey Forest in Ubud and interact with the playful monkeys.

36. Take a day trip to the nearby Nusa Islands for pristine beaches and crystal-clear waters.

37. Visit the Pura Ulun Danu Bratan Temple, located on the shores of Lake Bratan.

38. Attend a traditional Balinese gamelan.

39. Respect the culture and traditions of the local people.

40. Respect the religion of the locals.

41. Travel in a group rather than alone.

42. Pack a water bottle to stay hydrated.

43. Take antibiotics in case the local food doesn't suit you.

44. Learn a few local phrases.

45. Be careful of your belongings, and don't leave them unattended.

46. Make sure to lock your hotel room when leaving your things inside.

47. Don't display expensive items at all times.

48. Try local foods and enjoy Balinese cuisine.

49. Choose reputable restaurants to eat at.

50. Shop at the local markets.

51. Visit Bali's underwater aquarium restaurant called "Koral: Bali's First Aquarium Restaurant"

*Bali Travel Guide*

52. Ensure to brush your teeth with bottled water as tap water is not clean.

53. Do not have ice in drinks or anything to eat that would of been washed via the tap water

54. Use reputable taxi services and negotiate the fare before starting the trip.

55. Contemplate travelling during the shoulder season (April-May, September-October for fewer crowds and enjoyable weather

56. Treat the locals with respect

57. Always carry some cash in the local currency

58. Between July and October you can visit Kuta beach to watch baby sea turtles hatch on the beach at one of the conservation centres

59. Be cautious of pickpockets in crowded areas and keep your belongings secure.

60. Check the local calendar for important Balinese holidays or events that might impact your travel plans.

61. One of the more popular breakfast spots is "Crumb and Coaster"

62. 100,000 Indonesian Rupiah ($6.50 USD) is considered a large amount to Indonesian people so be sure not to over tip.

63. Airlines usually launch their discounts on Monday so look at Skyscanner on Tuesdays.

64. Carry a foldable rain poncho for unexpected rain showers especially when travelling in the wet season

65. Exchange currency at authorized money changers or banks to get the best rates.

66. Be cautious of stray dogs; avoid direct contact

67. Be cautious with street food; choose vendors with high turnover and where locals are eating to minimize risks.

68. Bali has an array of beach clubs to choose from

69. Traffic can be overcrowded, especially in popular areas like Kuta and Seminyak, be wary of this

70. In Bali, the socket used is a "type C". Buy a universal adapter according to this

71. Try to avoid spirits as much as possible. Cocktails/Spirits in Bali have been known to contain methanol.

72. If you plan on getting a tattoo in Bali, ensure you do your research and go to a parlour where the needles are sterile. Some parlours do not use sterile needles.

73. In Bali, you can get an IV drip if hungover/sunburnt or feeling unwell. For a fee, they will come to your hotel/villa and set up the drip for you.

74. There is a severe punishment for possession of narcotics in Indonesia. Steer well clear of people trying to sell you narcotics on the street.

75. "Gets your Guide" is a good app/website to use for booking activities

76. If trekking Mount Agung, hire a certified guide for safety and navigation.

77. Do not feed the monkeys at the monkey forest to avoid aggressive behaviour

78. Be careful of loose items around the monkeys as they will try to steal them

79. Use reef-safe sunscreen to protect Bali's coral reefs while enjoying water activities.

*Bali Travel Guide*

80. The air at the Balinese Volcanos is very pure. Balinese air is quite polluted so you will find the air very fresh upon going up one of their volcanos.

81. Visit [Kupu-Kupu Foundation Shop](#) to see a collection of art made by people with disabilities.

82. Visit Balinese orphanages for a wholesome experience

83. Use the taxi drivers' knowledge! I recommend getting in a reputable taxi and informing the driver of what you would like to do for the day. Then ask him to be your driver for the day and take you to the best spots he knows.

84. Explore the Bamboo Forest in Ubud

85. Take part in a bamboo weaving workshop to learn the art of creating intricate crafts using bamboo.

86. Make the effort to go to Mount Batur for sunrise for stunning views of the island from the summit

87. Visit the Bali Reptile Park to learn about the island's diverse reptile species

88. Highly recommend visiting The Dirty Duck Diner

89. Enjoy a calm canoeing experience at Lake Tamblingan

90. Join a dolphin watching tour at Lovina Beach where you will see the marine mammals in their natural habitat

91. Check to see if your resort or villa has the famous "floating breakfast" option

92. There are many quad biking tours you can do in Bali, research and find one best tailored to you

93. Recommend making the trip to Gitgit Waterfall

94. Try to explore as much of the island as possible! There is loads to do in Bali try to explore the island to get the most out of it

95. Enjoy a scenic walk along Campuhan Ridge
96. Check out Tanjung Benoa watersports
97. Visit the Taman Ujung water palace
98. Explore the abandoned Boeing 737 in Bukit Peninsula
99. Visit Upside Down World Bali
100. There are plenty of museum options in Bali! Research into your options if it piques your interested

# References

*A Guide to the Holy Springs of Tirta Empul: Bali's Sacred Water Temple*. (n.d.). Indonesia Travel. https://www.indonesia.travel/gb/en/destinations/bali-nusa-tenggara/bali/the-holy-springs-of-tirta-empul

*Adjusting to the culture in Bali - Guide*. (n.d.). Expat. https://www.expat.com/en/guide/asia/indonesia/bali/21563-adjusting-to-the-culture-in-bali.html

*Bali*. (n.d.). Travel Doctor-TMV C-TMVC. https://www.traveldoctor.com.au/destinations/bali

*Bali - History and Culture*. (n.d.). iExplore. https://www.iexplore.com/articles/travel-guides/south-and-southeast-asia/indonesia/bali/history-and-culture#:~:text=Even%20in%20its%20early%20years,the%20island%20became%20predominantly%20Hindu

Bali Emergency Numbers - Ambulance, Police, Fire. (n.d.). Bali.com. Retrieved August 21, 2023, from https://bali.com/bali/travel-guide/health-safety/emergency-numbers/

*Bali Geography*. (n.d.). Travel Online. https://www.travelonline.com/bali/geography

Bali Respect. (n.d.). Ubud Community. https://ubudcommunity.com/bali-respect/

*Bali Safari park review after 2023*. (2022, October 30). Tale Travels. https://www.taletravels.com/indonesia/bali-safari-park-review/

Brown, S. (2015, February 10). *6 dishes every visitor to Bali needs to taste*. CNN. https://edition.cnn.com/travel/article/balinese-dishes-cnngo/index.html

92

Caf, K. (2023). *Is There Uber in Bali in 2023? Grab & Gojek Uber Alternatives Guide*. Katie Caf Travel. https://www.katie-caftravel.com/uber-in-bali-and-getting-around-bali/#:~:text=travel%20in%20Bali.-,Uber%20Alternatives%3A%20Using%20Gojek%20%26%20Grab%20Apps%20In%20Bali,known%20as%20%E2%80%9CSuper%20Apps%E2%80%9D.

Carissa, V. (2023, April 6). *Shopping Places in Bali - Spots for Shop Till You Drop*. Villa Carissa Bali - Seminyak Center. https://www.villacarissabali.com/shop-till-you-drop-best-places-to-go-shopping-in-bali/

Charlotte. (2023). *East Bali guide: Top 11 awesome things to do*. Sunshine Seeker. https://www.sunshineseeker.com/indonesia/bali/east-bali-things-to-do/

*Climbing Mount Rinjani from Gili Trawangan*. (2018, November 8). Villas Edenia. https://villas-edenia.com/mount-rinjani-gili-trawangan/

Conn, K. (2023). *Things to Do in West Bali: A Road Trip Itinerary + Travel Guide*. Adventures and Sunsets. https://www.adventuresnsunsets.com/things-to-do-in-west-bali-road-trip-guide/#google_vignette

Cook, T. (2023). *Best Time to Visit Bali*. International Tourism. https://www.thomascook.in/international-tourism/best-time-to-visit-bali#:~:text=The%20best%20time%20to%20visit,in%20those%20mid%2Dseason%20months

*11 Best Nightlife Experiences in Legian - Where to Go and What to Do at Night in Legian - Go Guides*., (2023). Hotels.com. https://au.hotels.com/go/indonesia/best-legian-nightlife

Exquisite, & Media, E. (2020, July 17). *The Rich Flavours of Bali.* Exquisite Taste. https://exquisite-taste-magazine.com/rich-flavours-bali/

*5 UNIQUE PLACES TO STAY IN BALI.* (2022, July 22). The Asia Collective. https://theasiacollective.com/unique-places-to-stay-bali/

Greta. (2020, April 6). *33 BEST Bali Instagram Spots - The Most Photogenic Places In Bali.* Greta's Travels. https://gretastravels.com/bali-instagram-spots/

Gunadi, A. (n.d.). *Tanah Lot Temple in Bali.* Hotels.com. https://www.hotels.com/go/indonesia/tanah-lot-temple

Gurnani, S. (2021, December 1). *A Visit To This Elephant Safari Park In Ubud Will Make Your Trip To Indonesia More Funtastic.* Travel Triangle. https://traveltriangle.com/blog/elephant-safari-park-north-ubud/

Hajra, N. (n.d.). *Best Places to Stay in South Bali.* All Indonesia Travel. https://allindonesiatravel.com/best-areas-to-stay-south-central-bali/

*Indonesia - Traveler view | Travelers' Health.* (n.d.). CDC. https://wwwnc.cdc.gov/travel/destinations/traveler/none/indonesia

Intan, D. &. (2023, August 3). *Mason Elephant Sanctuary Bali: The Bali Elephant Rescue Park.* The World Travel Guy. https://theworldtravelguy.com/elephant-sanctuary-bali-mason-elephant-bali-park-lodge/

It's Me-Time: what to expect at a Bali spa. (2019, March 5). Pentravel Blog. https://blog.pentravel.co.za/its-me-time-what-to-expect-at-a-bali-spa/#:~:text=Bali%20spas%20fast%20facts%3A&text=Full%20body%20massages%20are%20the

Julie, C. (2022). *Balinese Traditions and Customs – A Cultural Guide*. South East-Asia Backpacker. https://southeastasiabackpacker.com/culture-bali/

*Ku De Ta Bali - Upscale Beachside Dining and Nightlife in Seminyak – Go Guides.* (2023). Hotels.com. https://www.hotels.com/go/indonesia/ku-de-ta-bali

*Local markets in Bali: The best spots to shop art, food, clothing & more!* (2022, August 8). Honeycombers Bali. https://thehoneycombers.com/bali/local-markets-in-bali/

Louise. (2023). *26 best beaches in Bali: Where to swim, surf, soak up the sun and live the island dream*. The HoneyCombers. https://thehoneycombers.com/bali/best-beach-bali-swim-surf-sand/

Macatulad, A. J. (2019, July 4). *14 Bali Restaurants You'll Want to Fly For*. Will Fly for Food. https://www.willflyforfood.net/bali-food-guide-14-must-eat-restaurants-in-ubud-seminyak/

Macatulad, A. J. (2022, October 20). *Balinese Food: 10 Dishes You Need to Try in Bali*. Will Fly for Food. https://www.willflyforfood.net/balinese-food/

Macrae, I. W. (n.d.). *Insights on Balinese Linguistic Analysis*. academia.edu. Retrieved August 22, 2023, from https://www.academia.edu/36642331/Insights_on_Balinese_Linguistic_Analysis

Marlin. (2023). *Driving in Bali: Rules, Requirements, and Safety Tips*. Travelepsy. https://travelepsy.com/indonesia/driving-bali#google_vignette

*Mason Elephant Park- Mason Adventures (Bali Adventure Tours)*. (n.d.). Mason Adventures. https://www.masonadventures.com/elephant-park/

Matt. (n.d.). *Transportation in Bali, The 9 Best Ways to Get Around*. Greener Bali. https://greenerbali.com/bali-transportation/#google_vignette

Michael. (2022). *Do I need a Visa to get into Bali?* Bali Holiday Secrets. https://www.baliholidaysecrets.com/visa-bali/

Michelle. (2023, May 30). *29 Best Restaurants In Bali For Legit Balinese Food, Cave Dining, And More.* Eatbook.sg. https://eatbook.sg/best-restaurants-bali/

Milijana, A. (2019, March 21). *Borobudur vs Prambanan: Epic Borobudur and Prambanan temples.* World Travel Connector. https://www.worldtravelconnector.com/sunrise-tour-borobudur-blog-prambanan-temple-yogyakarta-indonesia/#:~:text=While%20Borobudur%20is%20a%20Buddhist

Move, B. on the. (2022, January 18). *Ultimate Guide To Shopping In Bali For Tourists Ultimate Guide To Shopping In Bali For Tourists.* Brit on the MoveTM. https://britonthemove.com/shopping-in-bali-for-tourists/

Nick and Hannah (2023, April 18). *8 Best Places to Stay In Bali: Top Areas and Hotels.* Salt in Our Hair Travel Blog. https://www.saltinourhair.com/bali/best-places-stay-bali/

Pack Your Bags: Packing List for Bali. (n.d.). Bali Travel Guide. https://bali.com/bali/travel-guide/practical-tips-must-know/packing-list-suitcase/

Pauly, C. (2020, January 29). *Waterbom Bali In Kuta - A Complete Guide.* Charlie Pauly. https://charliepauly.com/waterbom-bali/

Pauly, C. (2023, June 10). *50 Most Instagrammable Places In Bali.* Charlie Pauly. https://charliepauly.com/bali-instagram-spots/

Putradana. (2022). *History About Why is Bali Called the island of Gods.* E-Visa Info. https://www.evisabali.com/2022/10/21/history-about-why-is-bali-called-the-island-of-gods/

Rose. (2023). *Exploring Bali Arts: Preserving the Island's Rich Cultural Legacy.* Hindi Rocks. https://hindirocks.com/balinese-traditional-arts-and-crafts-preserving-cultural-heritage/

SHEPPARD, A. (2022, April 22). *10 Best Luxury Wellness Retreats In Bali For A Luxury Island Retreat [Review of 10 Best Luxury Wellness Retreats In Bali For A Luxury Island Retreat].* Compare Retreats. https://magazine.compareretreats.com/best-wellness-retreats-in-bali/

*Surf vacations and balinese spa: massage, body scrub and other treatments.* (2017, January 30). WaveHouse. https://wavehouse-bali.com/balinese-spa/

Tanja. (2022, November 27). *How to homestay in Bali.* Please Be Seated for Takeoff. https://pleasebeseatedfortakeoff.com/how-to-homestay-in-bali/#:~:text=Homestay%20simply%20means%20staying%20in

10 Best Places for Yoga/Meditation in Bali | Solo Female Travel - Unbounded Swagachi. (2021, July 10). Swagachi. https://swagachi.me/yoga-meditation-solo-female-travel-bali/

Teslaru, A. (2021, February 22). *Crystal Bay Beach, Nusa Penida - An EPIC travel guide.* Daily Travel Pill. https://dailytravelpill.com/crystal-bay-beach-nusa-penida/

Thalpe, W. (2023, March 22). *Culture and Traditions in Bali: Money, Gestures, Table Manners & Religion [Review of Culture and Traditions in Bali: Money, Gestures, Table Manners & Religion].* LinkedIn. https://www.linkedin.com/pulse/culture-traditions-bali-money-gestures-table-manners-religion-thalpe/

Tourists in Bali? Stay Prepared with Hospital Contact and Hotline Information. (2023, June 12). Social Expat. https://www.socialexpat.net/tourists-in-bali-stay-prepared-with-hospital-contact-and-hotline-information/

Travioor. (2017, January 11). *6 of the Best Bars in Bali for a Pub Crawl.* Medium. https://medium.com/@travioor/6-of-the-best-bars-in-bali-for-a-pub-crawl-fb77824c202e

Turtle, M. (2023). *The Force is Strong*. Time Travel Turtle. https://www.timetravelturtle.com/the-force-is-strong/

*29 Best Nightlife in Seminyak - Best Places to Go at Night in Seminyak - Go Guides.*, (2023). Hotels.com. https://au.hotels.com/go/indonesia/best-seminyak-nightlife

*20 Common Bali Scams and how to avoid the scams.* (2023, January 10). Girlswanderlust. https://girlswanderlust.com/20-tourist-traps-bali-scams/#:~:text=Paying%20for%20photoWayan. (2023, July 18). *Balinese Words and Phrases: 79 To Use Instantly! Taman Dukuh Bali Farm Cooking School | Cooking Class Ubud.* https://tamandukuh.com/balinese-words-and-meanings/

Printed in Great Britain
by Amazon